D1559322

ALSO BY **KIRK MARTIN**

Shade of the Maple

The Gravel Drive

Gifted

www.kirkmartinbooks.com

*Celebrate!*ADHD

Kirk & Anita Martin

CANTWELL-HAMILTON PRESS

CANTWELL-HAMILTON PRESS

43192 Newbridge Square
Washington, D.C. 20148

The information in this book is not intended as a substitute for consultation with a healthcare professional. Each individual's health concerns should be evaluated by a qualified professional.

For more information, please visit us on the web.
www.CelebrateADHD.com
ADHDcamp@aol.com

Cover design by Lee Lewis, Words Plus Design
www.wordsplusdesign.com

Manufactured in the United States of America

10   9   8   7   6   5   4   3   2   1

Library of Congress Cataloging-in-Publication Data
Martin, Kirk and Anita. 1966-
  Celebrate! ADHD / Kirk and Anita Martin.
    p.   cm.

  1. Attention-deficit hyperactivity disorder—Popular works.
  2. Child rearing—Popular works.

ISBN 0-9716145-3-9

Dedication

This book is dedicated to the amazing children who have touched our lives, energized our spirits and transformed our souls.

Contents

FOREWORD   Howard Glasser

I.   INTRODUCTION: INSIDE THE HEAD   15
        AND HEART OF A CHILD WITH ADHD

II.   10 ATTITUDES THAT DESTROY A CHILD'S   21
        CONFIDENCE, PURPOSE AND JOY

       # 1   There is Something Wrong with You   27

       # 2   Swimming in a Sea of Negativity   39

       # 3   The Little Train That Couldn't   45

       # 4   Ignoring Gifts, Talents and Passions   50

       # 5   Demanding Success in Every Subject   54

       # 6   Using School as a Predictor of Success   60
                 in the Real World

       # 7   Fighting Their Own Nature   68

       # 8   Changing Our Child, Instead of Ourselves   71

       # 9   Trusting Experts Rather Than Parents   77

       # 10   Feeding Children a Diet of Disapproval   81

Contents

III.   10 REASONS WE CELEBRATE! ADHD   85

    # 1   Think Different, Wonderfully Different   88

    # 2   Celebrate the Trailblazer Under Your Roof   92

    # 3   Leverage Competitive Advantages   99

    # 4   Capitalize on Future Trends   103

    # 5   Turn Negatives into Positives   107

    # 6   Cultivate Your Child's Natural Gifts, Talents and Passions   120

    # 7   Craft a Vision with Large Goals   135

    # 8   Live with Purpose   139

    # 9   Identify and Overcome Obstacles   142

    # 10   Encourage Healthy Relationships   145

    CREATE YOUR ACTION PLAN   154

IV.   10 STRATEGIES TO IMPROVE YOUR CHILD'S SCHOOL EXPERIENCE   157

    ACKNOWLEDGMENTS   171

Foreword

Living or dying by one's fire.

It feels very fitting that I'm writing this Foreword on Independence Day. I can only imagine that there are infinite levels of true independence that transcend our traditional ways of celebrating July Fourth.

One such way of achieving independence is discovering who we really are and becoming all we can be. Reclaiming our divine inheritance may be the one noble task of our lifetime.

A long time ago, I was struck by a quote that hit me like a ton of bricks: "A person either lives by his fire or dies by his fire."

Children who are unfairly labeled and discouraged because they fit the preconceived profile of the medical community are particularly prone to such self-destruction.

So many of these children come to fear their intensity and subsequently divorce themselves from the very fire that fuels their creativity and dreams. I can't think of anything sadder. And if we don't have systematic ways to fan the flames of their greatness, we stand to lose yet more generations of the best and brightest.

The sad truth is that many of our potentially best, brightest and most creative children don't make it. They get lost in the shuffle, unable to get past the doubts to truly believe in themselves, and unable to find the independence that unlocks the magic of life. Unfortunately, too many of our children feel most celebrated when they are doing the wrong things— because that's when adults give them their time and energy.

Celebrate! ADHD honors the work of *The Nurtured Heart Approach* by cultivating each child's inner wealth and self-worth—and for that I am so grateful.

More importantly, **Celebrate! ADHD** nurtures each child's inner strength and emerging experience of success even further.

This wonderful work of Kirk and Anita Martin will help transform the deflating experiences children encounter at home and school into a celebration of their natural gifts, talents and passions. This positive affirmation produces success—not just ordinary levels of success, but rousing levels of success.

From their unique vantage point, the Martins provide **10 Reasons to Celebrate ADHD,** and show us how to bring magic to our children's everyday experiences. I celebrate this book and its contribution to helping children fulfill their great destinies.

The powerful methods presented in **Celebrate! ADHD** help these children feel so valued that they flourish into who they are destined to be. Feeling a deep, abiding sense of self-confidence and acceptance leads to true independence—an inner independence that fuels their fire and helps them accomplish extraordinary things in their lifetime.

I implore you to **Celebrate! ADHD.**

Howard Glasser
Tucson, AZ
July 4, 2005

Celebrate!ADHD

I.

Introduction: Inside the Head & Heart of A Child with ADHD

WHAT IT'S LIKE TO BE A CHILD WITH ADHD

Dear Mom and Dad,

I want you to know what it's like to be me.

My brain runs like a washing machine powered by a Ferrari engine. It runs all the time and it runs fast, churning and tumbling ideas like shirts and pants and socks mixed together.

I can be talking to you and having another conversation running inside my head. I can be in class listening to the teacher, but be fully engaged in a daydream or hearing a new song on my guitar.

You know how I sometimes repeat questions? It's not that I didn't hear your answer. It's just that in the second between the time I asked and you responded, I went somewhere interesting in my mind. And I didn't pay attention to what you said.

Sometimes I have so many thoughts swimming inside my head that I just blurt things out because I'm afraid I will forget them.

I want to do well in school. But when the teacher drones on and doesn't engage my imagination, either my mind shuts down to sleep mode or I tune her out and go to better places that keep me stimulated. It's nothing personal.

I kind of like all this energy inside my head because I can keep myself engaged and entertained in there by myself. But other times I feel scattered.

That's why I like routine in other parts of life. It's why I end up wearing or eating the same things. I don't need variety with most things because I have so much variety inside my head.

You think I'm sad because I don't have lots of friends. But that's by choice, because I'm pretty content inside.

I like who I am, but it's tough when no one else seems to. Why does everyone want to change who I am? You give me medication to make me a different person, a person I don't care to be. I'm not unhappy with myself—I'm uneasy because since I can remember, everyone around me has been so negative and tried to fix what they think is wrong with me.

You want me to talk more, but you just psychoanalyze me. Besides, it's difficult to express my thoughts and feelings verbally—they just get jumbled up. I'd rather express them in my writing and music. I feel things deeply. I hurt with the kids who get left out, and one day I'm going to help those kids. I know how it feels.

I know you get concerned because I stay up late at night and don't sleep much. But I like it when it's quiet. I can hear my thoughts better. And my world is peaceful then.

Mom and Dad, don't worry about me. I may not do great in school or be the most popular kid, but I'm content inside. I like the way my brain works, I like my energy. If everyone would stop trying to fix me, I'd be okay.

Let me focus on the things I love doing. Writing songs, playing music. Stop trying to make me be like everyone else. Just work with me, okay, not against me. I like who I am. Why can't you?

THIS BOOK WILL HELP YOU IF...

Your child needs confidence and a strong self-identity.

Your child has difficulty developing healthy friendships.

Your child struggles in school, even though he is very bright.

You want to eliminate or reduce your child's dependence on medication.

Your family has spiraled out of control into an explosive household—ripped apart by stress, conflict and tension.

You have spent countless hours and dollars having your child diagnosed by therapists, psychologists and learning specialists.

You feel guilty because you are beginning to view your child as the problem.

Your child has begun to utter negative self-talk.

You worry that your child will not be able to enjoy a successful career and a stable family.

You know there's a better way to help your child. You want a positive, proactive approach that focuses on your child's gifts instead of his weaknesses.

You've somehow lost your perspective…and just want your happy little boy or girl back.

HOW IS THIS BOOK DIFFERENT?

Contrary to those whose perspective of ADHD is pessimistic—and at times fatalistic—we enthusiastically celebrate the natural gifts, talents and passions of children with ADHD.

We provide positive, proactive solutions to restore confidence, improve relationships and reduce the anxiety of children with ADHD.

This book is purposefully concise and written in an ADHD-friendly format. There is plenty of white space. Text is confined to short blocks of information.

This book is about personal responsibility—expressing gratitude for the clay you've been given and practicing stewardship by shaping lives full of promise.

Do not allow yourself to be relegated to the sidelines. Jump in with both feet, take charge and let's forge a path together toward a meaningful future for you and your family!

First, we will challenge old assumptions and review the attitudes that harm our children. In the second half of the book, we will develop an Action Plan to restore your child's confidence, purpose and joy.

II.

10 Attitudes That Destroy Our Child's Confidence, Purpose & Joy

WHY DO WE DO THIS TO OUR CHILDREN?

1. Parents, teachers and therapists spend a child's early years echoing a constant chorus: "There is something wrong with you"…and then wonder why they lack self-confidence.

2. We force our kids to swim in a sea of negativity…and wonder why they feel anxious and depressed.

3. We continually focus on what children with ADHD cannot do…and then wonder why they are confused and directionless.

4. We ignore or dismiss our kids' natural gifts and talents—because they don't fit *our* narrow definition of success—and then wonder why they are apathetic.

5. We demand academic success in every subject, even though schools exploit our children's weaknesses …and wonder why they are overwhelmed with anxiety.

6. We establish success in school as the predictor of success in life, judging our kids' performance against an artificial standard…and wonder why they have no hope.

7. We ask our children to fight their own nature, to do things they cannot do no matter how hard they try…and wonder why they are frustrated and angry.

8. We try to change our children—through pressure and medication—instead of changing the way we teach or view them…and then wonder why they lack a strong identity.

9. We cede care of our children to "experts" with an endless chorus of diagnoses rather than trusting our own instincts as parents…and then wonder why our kids no longer respond to us.

10. We feed our kids a constant diet of scorn and disapproval…and then wonder why they seek positive affirmation and a sense of belonging from other disaffected kids.

A PEEK INSIDE A REAL THIRD GRADE CLASSROOM...

As you wind along the tree-covered lanes of Brookfield, Wisconsin, you see the boundless optimism in hundreds of children scurrying into Chestnut Hills Elementary. It's a brand new school, built to support the booming suburbs of this chilly city. An American flag bristles in the wind and a granite sign welcomes you to the *Home of the Badgers*.

You walk through the sparkling lobby. Crayon pictures flap in the hallway. Everything seems so miniature—the lockers, the water fountains, the hallways. You turn a corner and find the third grade classroom, home to Ms. Saunders and her thirty students. You peek inside and this is what you see.

Jimmy Sullivan feels lost. The days of carefree innocence that should be the right of every eight-year-old have been shattered. He's heard the whispers and the four-letter word his doctor mutters: ADHD. He cuddles into his fleece sweatshirt and stares out the window. He can't recall information very quickly and gets frustrated taking tests. All he knows is that he's trying. He really is.

Behind him sits **Allison Jennings**. In her little world, she is a singer and entertainer, a Drama Queen of epic proportions. She's always singing, humming, banging on something, anything to make "music" that others hear as "noise." It drives her Mom crazy. Allison has grown immune to her mother's constant pleadings, "Can't you just be quiet for once?" When her Mom asks if she's taken her medication, Allison wonders inside why everyone wants her to be different.

Across the room, **Mikey Williams** is busy gazing at a picture book instead of listening to Ms. Saunders. He sees her lips moving, but can't put the words together. He senses the world in colorful pictures and big ideas. He is fascinated by rockets and airplanes, but Ms. Saunders doesn't talk about the things he's interested in. He tunes her out and anxiously waits for the day to end so he can run home and build his model airplanes. He's actually quite good at building, his father muses, just wish he'd pay attention and do better in school.

Shawn Gillespie is hard at work, intently focused on his project while Ms. Saunders is instructing the class. He switches crayons and his hand races across the poster board. Shawn is unaware that the teacher is now standing behind him. "What are you doing, Shawn?" Ms. Saunders snaps. His classmates giggle. Shawn looks up innocently. "I'm making a couple of signs for a yard sale this weekend to earn some money," he replies earnestly. It isn't his assignment. He always seems to be on another page.

Laurie Daniels is staring out the window, lost in an elaborate tale that runs vividly through her mind. It seems more real than reality itself, and as she reaches for her # 2 pencil and some clean paper, she hears Ms. Saunders ask a question. She sits frozen, embarrassed. She knows she's different. Maybe that's why she sees three different therapists after school every week. Maybe that's why she doesn't have many friends. Her teachers and parents are concerned because she seems so pensive and distant in thought. Their tone says there is something wrong with her, but she feels perfectly content within. Why doesn't anyone else understand?

Robert and Susan Taggart are fighting again in the hallway while they wait for class to dismiss. They've assured their children it isn't about them, but Aaron, the middle child, knows better. They know he is intelligent, perhaps the brightest of their three children. So why won't he pay attention, why doesn't he get better grades? They are tired of fighting, exhausted at trying everything to prod Aaron. They pressure him from morning to bedtime. They are afraid their love has turned to bitterness and resentment. The constant frustration and tension is tearing their family apart. Maybe the teacher can help.

Ms. Saunders has devoted her life to helping children learn. She fights to retain her youthful idealism. She not only has thirty students with different learning styles and needs, she has thirty sets of parents with their own expectations. Her heart breaks for the children with ADHD. She wants to individualize her lessons, but she can't. There is no guidebook for this, she hasn't been taught how to manage such a diverse group. And the school doesn't have the resources to meet all the needs of children with learning difficulties. She's doing her best.

DO YOU RECOGNIZE ANY OF THESE KIDS?
If so, you are not alone. Millions of families have spun out of control, desperate for answers. Fortunately, our solutions are derived from common sense.

First, we must recognize the attitudes that are hurting our children. The truth is that your attitude toward your child will have a greater impact on his life than anything else. Then, we can act with compassion to chart a hopeful and bright course for the future.

1 THERE IS SOMETHING WRONG WITH YOU

Parents, teachers and therapists spend a child's early years echoing a constant chorus: "There is something wrong with you"... and then wonder why they lack self-confidence.

There is something wrong with you.

Can you imagine a phrase more debilitating to the fragile confidence of a little boy or girl? And yet it's the phrase that welcomes millions of young children to school. A college-aged girl named Julie recounted this story to us:

> I remember being so excited that my parents were coming to meet my second grade teacher, Mrs. Tanner. I wore my best dress and was on my best behavior.
>
> When my parents stepped through the door, I could see they weren't smiling. I ran and hugged my Dad. I felt his big, gentle hand patting my head as I held onto his leg.
>
> Mrs. Tanner escorted us to an office. All I remember was the somber look on her face. I played with my doll while the grown-ups talked quietly. The next time I looked up, my Mom was crying and my Dad was silent.
>
> And then I heard my teacher utter the words that changed my life. "We need to do some testing to determine what is wrong with her."

There's something wrong with me.

I sure didn't feel like there was. I was a pretty happy kid until that day. I adored my parents and my little brother, not to mention my dog and kitten.

But from that point on, everyone treated me like there was something wrong with me. I never felt quite right about myself after that.

I'D RATHER HAVE STICKS AND STONES BREAK MY BONES...

People with the symptoms of ADHD have been called lazy, dumb, slow, retarded, disruptive, impossible, stupid and bad. At one time, they were even labeled "brain damaged."

But these names have been replaced by an even more insidious label. Listen to Corey tell his story. At 14, Corey is a phenomenal piano player. Though he is clearly gifted, until recently he never had the confidence to play for others.

> You know that saying, "Sticks and stones may break my bones, but words will never hurt me?" Well, that's stupid. When you are told everyday—whether it's in a teacher's eyes or your parents' fights—that there is something wrong with you, it hurts.

> It made me think I could never do anything right, so I stopped trying. I'd rather have sticks and stones break my bones. At least you can fix a broken bone. But how do you fix a broken spirit?

RIGHT LETTER, WRONG WORD
Every day, thousands of students receive the Scarlet D around their neck.

A disorder is a condition in which there is a disturbance of normal functioning.

We've gotten the letter correct. "D."

But the correct word is not "disorder." Labeling with a disorder means there is something inherently *wrong* or *abnormal* with your genetic make-up. Like you can never fix it. It drives the feeling of inferiority deep inside, making you think something inside you needs to be fixed.

The correct word is "different."

The tone of this book is an unapologetic celebration of the many advantages people with ADHD have because of their unique (dare we say, "different") gifts, passions and skills.

We categorically reject the misdirected pity or victimization placed upon us by such labels. And we enthusiastically embrace a proactive approach to capitalize on these unique skills in order to restore confidence, purpose and joy in children who have been labeled with ADHD.

JEANS MAY FADE, BUT GENES DON'T LIE

Let's begin by acknowledging a truth everyone can agree with. People's brains work in unique and perceptibly different ways.

Some are listeners.	Others are doers.
Some like executing details.	Others are energized by ideas.
Some recall facts quickly.	Others graze on information.
Some need stability.	Others enjoy risk.
Some prefer the status quo.	Others are change-agents.
Some are methodical thinkers.	Others are intuitive feelers.
Some are compliant.	Others are defiant, persistent.
Some work well in groups.	Others work independently.
Some are managers.	Others are creators.

Is there an inherent superiority—and hence inferiority—of a certain genetic make-up? Absolutely not. Different vocations require different strengths.

The fact is that ADHD is a genetic difference that predisposes some people to have difficulty with executive function and quick recall, but predisposes them to excel in an unstructured environment that requires creativity, risk-taking and intuition.

YOU CAN'T TELL ONLY HALF THE STORY

Consider 16-year-old Morgan Kazulo. Like many kids with ADHD, he often has difficulty listening, following instructions, organizing, staying on task, exerting mental focus for extended periods, recalling information in short-term memory files, and processing spoken information (auditory processing).

If you stop at this point and never consider Morgan's strengths, then you may conclude that his brain is "abnormal."

But you cannot stop there. This debilitating obsession with perceived negatives is more harmful than the symptoms of ADHD.

If all you told your children about World War II was the bombing of Pearl Harbor and the Nazi conquest of Europe, they would think we lost the war. It's like telling your kids that Lance Armstrong had cancer spread through his lungs and brain…but failing to emphasize the positive news: he not only recovered, he won a record number of Tour de France races.

We cannot tell only half the story about children with ADHD. We should be mindful of their weaknesses, but never forget to celebrate their natural gifts, talents and passions.

And now the rest of the story. Morgan Kazulo is an internationally recognized violinist who has developed an innovative program to help disadvantaged children. If his brain is abnormal, then we need more kids like him.

IS THERE "SOMETHING WRONG"?
So are you saying that there isn't anything wrong with kids with ADHD?

There is something wrong with all of us.

Point out 100 strangers and I will show you 100 people with deficiencies and weaknesses galore. The erudite professor lacks common sense, doesn't understand basic principles of personal finance and has failed relationships. The accomplished businessman cannot fix his car, write a song or speak with humility. The brilliant scientist has no leadership skills, is afraid to take risks and doesn't have a creative bone in his body.

The most intelligent and studied among us may not be able to write a screenplay, direct a movie, act on Broadway, sing a song, start a business, design an advertising campaign, invent a new product, work in an unstructured environment or bounce back with resilience after failure. Does that mean they are abnormal?

People with ADHD have real obstacles to overcome. But who doesn't?

WHO DECIDES WHAT IS NORMAL?

Who decides which qualities are more important than others?

- When you need someone to manage a complex business, you look for someone who is organized, enjoys executing details and can complete dozens of tasks consistently.

- When you need someone to start a new business, you look for someone who is creative, innovative, challenges norms, is prone to action and not afraid of risk.

- When you need someone to entertain people, you look for someone with a gift for the performing arts—whether it's playing music, singing, acting, writing or painting.

Are any of these skill sets inherently superior to the others? Absolutely not. They are just different.

STRANGERS IN A STRANGE LAND

Christopher Campbell hops out of his Mom's car, slings a backpack over his shoulder and bounds into Chestnut Hills Elementary. He looks forward to school, enjoys the challenges and seems to flourish within these halls. He completes his assignments on time, asks for extra homework and remains one of his teacher's favorites. After school, the baseball diamond calls his name and he plays hard until the sun goes down.

He checks in at the office, obtains his pass for being late after a doctor's appointment, then proceeds down the empty hallway toward his classroom. He opens the door and is stunned. Ms. Saunders waves a friendly hello and returns to her work. The right teacher, he says to himself, but this classroom sure looks different. Not like his regular third grade classroom.

The desks are not arranged in orderly rows. The lesson plan isn't written on the chalkboard. He walks into the room tentatively, unsure where to put his books and lunch. Canvasses, beanbag chairs and laptops are scattered across the room. Some kids are painting, some writing, others tapping away at computer keyboards and still others building elaborate airplane models. The room is open and uncluttered, with plenty of sunlight and brightly colored walls.

His classmates are working independently on their own projects. Some listen to iPods, some sit quietly and work. None of them are distracted by him walking into the room—they are absorbed in their work, intense concentration in their eyes. He notices that most of the kids are wearing baggy, comfortable clothes.

"Good morning, Christopher," Ms. Saunders says with a smile. "Why don't you go ahead and begin working on your project?"

Christopher stares back at his teacher blankly. He appears lost, unsure whether he should ask questions for fear of looking stupid or just sit down. He finds an empty chair. He fumbles through his books and glances around, alternately feeling out of place, bored and directionless. He can't wait for the bell to ring and class to be over. He doesn't belong here, he mutters to himself.

That night, his parents find a note from Ms. Saunders in his backpack:

Dear Mr. and Mrs. Campbell,

Please call me at your earliest convenience so we may speak about Christopher. I am concerned about his behavior. He doesn't seem to pay attention nor does he appear interested in his project. His eyes wander about the room, he seems to be elsewhere. Instead of working on his project independently like everyone else, he roams around and invariably disrupts his classmates.

Christopher doesn't show much initiative in class. I had to prompt him to paint a landscape. When he did, his brushstrokes were uneven and perspective skewed, showing an utter lack of creativity.

I then coaxed Christopher to write a story, any story. He sat with a blank look on his face and said he couldn't think of anything to write about. I'm concerned about his poor imagination—it shows a lack of cognitive interest and curiosity. Though we've covered these concepts in class, Christopher appears unable to comprehend the importance of character development and conflict within a story.

In fact, when I opened his notebook to review his assignment, I found that he had not worked on his writing project. Instead, he had been doing complex math problems in class. While impressed by his mathematical abilities, this was neither the time nor place for that.

I then had to prompt him to try another creative exercise. The other children lead effortlessly, work independently and show initiative quite well. Christopher seems to need more hand-holding and constant instruction than should be necessary. I'm afraid he's energy deficient.

I am also concerned because he doesn't understand proper social cues in interactions with classmates. Christopher seems unaware of other students' needs for privacy and concentration when they are writing, composing or drawing.

I have asked the school learning specialist and psychologist to join us for our meeting so that we may develop a plan to help Christopher succeed in school. After undergoing testing, we will be able to determine which combination of medication and behavior modification techniques will fix what's wrong with your son. He is capable of the work—he just needs some help.

Sincerely,

Jane Saunders

A RHETORICAL CHALLENGE

- Is there something "wrong" with Christopher?

- Does Christopher have a disorder?

- Christopher cannot paint, write or play music. Does that mean his brain is abnormal?

- Should his success in school be based solely on his ability to do things he isn't gifted at doing?

- Should the school system keep Christopher in this classroom and try to force him to be like everyone else, or should they give him opportunities to develop his strengths?

- Should Christopher take medication so that he will be able to think more creatively?

- Should teachers and parents try to change his genetic wiring and force him be a writer or performer?

Any reasonable, commonsense person will have the same answer to each of these questions.

Of course not.

Then why do we do the same exact thing to our kids?

STRAIGHT TALK

Most of the time, our kids are pretty content until we start labeling them. They are diagnosed with what is usually nothing more than a list of their natural weaknesses, and suddenly our sole focus is on what they cannot do well.

Our words, body language and attitude send this new message—there is something wrong with you. Is it any wonder our kids lack confidence and feel incapable?

Kids need a certain amount of inclusiveness, to feel like everyone else. To separate them so early in life from friends and the "normal" kids can leave permanent scars. While some kids don't mind being "different," they like to choose that label themselves, not have it placed upon them by someone else for differences they cannot control.

Parents, remember to keep perspective. Everyone has weaknesses. Focus on your child's strengths and determine which specific skills need to be improved.

Treat your child as a whole person, not merely as a collection of individual scores on aptitude tests. The sum of your child is not limited to certain academic capabilities in a classroom. They possess intangible qualities and character traits that often outweigh other deficiencies. Celebrate these positives.

How can we expect a child to like himself when everyone else sends the message that they don't like who he is? How can he form healthy relationships with others, when he doesn't have a healthy relationship with himself first?

2 SWIMMING IN A SEA OF NEGATIVITY

We force our kids to swim in a sea of negativity...
and wonder why they feel anxious and depressed.

The sun rises over the sleepy Pennsylvania hills. Evan rises as well, but not so brightly. The second-grader stumbles through his morning routine, nibbling on his waffles while muttering that he doesn't want to go to school.

He boards the crowded bus, quickly takes a seat by himself and stares out the window. It's already been a long day, he thinks. Butterflies churn inside as the elementary school comes into view. He walks down the hallway, opens his locker and realizes he has forgotten his language folder. The bell rings and his stomach tightens.

He looks up wearily as Miss Johnston passes out the assignment. He usually knows the answers, but what's in his brain doesn't make it to paper the right way. Or quickly enough. He gets distracted by noisy classmates and his own imagination. For a moment, he answers questions quickly, but then begins to struggle. Like he always does.

His teacher hovers over him. He gets even more distracted and nervous. He knows the material, but no one seems to care that the system is rigged against his nature— school favors those who work systematically, quickly and in a structured manner. When he can't complete his work on time, he misses recess. The negativity escalates.

All of a sudden, he's told that something is wrong with him. He doesn't *think* there's anything wrong with him. In fact, he's quite content inside. He has a vivid imagination, enjoys dreaming up stories and creating interesting characters. But then he feels the pressure. His teacher is scowling, his grades are bad, notes get sent home.

All day long, it's a struggle. Even the crowded, noisy lunchroom doesn't provide a reprieve. He gives his sandwich to a classmate, saving the brownies for himself. The final bell rings and he exhales. As he boards the bus, he is exhausted. Physically. Emotionally. Mentally. And it's only Tuesday.

He welcomes the sight of his house and runs from the bus. Time to relax and play outside with his dog and neighbors.

"How was your day today, Evan?" his mother asks.

"Fine. I'm going to Tommy's house."

"Not quite so fast, Evan. Miss Johnston called me this afternoon."

"Can't we talk about this later, Mom?"

The outside activities he needs in order to relax and expend his energy are put on hold. His well-meaning Mom insists that he do his homework before he can play. But he works slowly and his friends will be gone by the time he finishes. Evan erupts violently, throwing his books against the wall and calling his mother a "stupid jerk."

Tensions escalate. His mother is at her wit's end, shaking with anger and fear at what is happening to her son. And what is happening to her. She sends Evan to his room. He obliges with a slammed door.

Evan stares out the window. Life shouldn't be this tough. He wonders why he's like this, promises himself he'll do better. He walks tentatively down the stairs and asks his Mom for forgiveness. He asks when his father is going to be home. Maybe they can play catch before it gets dark.

He picks up his books and shuffles up to his room. An hour later, his father walks through the door and sees the look in his wife's eyes. "He's causing problems again, why does he have to be like this?" He marches up the stairs and asks his son what the problem is. He simply isn't buying this ADHD excuse. He knows his son is capable, he just needs to focus and make it work. Or no TV, Boy Scouts or football. His son sits and mumbles that it's really hard. "Yeah, well life is hard, son. But you have to do this. That's all there is to it."

Evan sits in his room, contemplating his life. His parents are on him 24/7. Last year, life was nothing but sunny days, peanut butter and jelly sandwiches and a bright future. Now every day is a struggle. Five days a week, he faces an increasingly scornful and disappointed teacher. Three days a week, he gets carted off to see a psychologist, a reading specialist and a speech therapist. He begins to believe the negative talk. Maybe there is something wrong with him. Maybe it's not worth it anymore—he doesn't know how to try any harder.

Negativity surrounds him. Everyone tells him what he can't do well, what his problems are and tries to fix what is wrong. No one takes the time to ask what he enjoys, focus on his strengths or let him be a kid.

And now home isn't even a respite. His Mom and Dad don't laugh anymore, just wear worried faces. He isn't sure his own parents like him now—he's the cause of the fighting.

As Evan grows older, the intensity only increases. He has to take medication to change who he is so that he can be successful. The constant scorn breeds anger and resentment.

He turns to a group of outcasts bitten by pain. He doesn't know their stories, why they seem so bitter and angry, doesn't care really. He just knows he feels at home with them because they share some kind of bond. Their future is as bleak as his.

Maybe they are right. There is something wrong with me. I don't care anymore.

A MILLION EVANS

Evan's story is common in millions of households across America. Maybe you recognize some of the same family dynamics. It doesn't take a psychologist or learning specialist to tell us the effects of constant negativity on a child—or anyone for that matter. Take a moment and put yourself in your child's shoes.

Count all the places and times he encounters negativity. Then count his positive experiences, the times he has heard affirmation or encouragement. You do the math. It's not difficult to understand the equation.

DESTRUCTIVE SELF-TALK

"I'm stupid." "I can't do anything right." "I hate myself." "I'm no good at school."

It is one thing for your child to pick up on the general feelings of negativity around him. But when destructive self-talk becomes internalized, it means your child is beginning to view the disorder as an inseparable part of who he is, to be defined by ADHD.

The purpose of this book is to prevent this insidious self-talk from happening in the first place, to proactively fill our children with hope based on a more well-rounded view of reality.

Our children are not the sum of what they cannot do. They are not one and the same with ADHD. But when that's what we make their life revolve around—instead of finding and feeding their passions and gifts—how can we expect a different result?

DOUBLE WHAMMY

Negativity hurts people with ADHD particularly severely. Why? Because children with ADHD tend to be sensitive and idealistic with a need for positive reinforcement. They do not possess the typical defense systems to reject others' negativity. It sticks to their bones. So they naturally repel people who are negative or douse their dreams.

This negativity permeating our attitudes has the exact opposite effect—it drives our kids further away. We need to provide our children with a safe place, to always believe in them and communicate a "can do" attitude even when they struggle.

Negative talk weakens their internal constitution. It is an offense to their idealism, an assault on their self-image.

DEFINING BY WEAKNESSES

Why do we focus ONLY on their weaknesses instead of valuing their competitive advantages and strengths?

In most cases when describing people, we begin by recounting their strengths or gifts. *He is an accomplished violinist. She is a real math whiz. He leads a Fortune 500 company. She has an amazing gift for decorating.* But when we describe people with ADHD, how do we begin? Right. With a list of what they cannot do.

Can you name another group of people we identify solely by their weaknesses?

Focusing on what someone cannot do—rather than what they can do—is <u>always</u> a recipe for failure, especially for kids with ADHD.

PROPHETS OF GLOOM AND DOOM

Nothing repulses us more than the constant diet of doom and gloom fed to people with ADHD. ADHD presents challenges, sometimes severe. And we understand the need to secure increased funding for helpful special education programs. But if you listen to most professionals speak about ADHD, you would swear they were describing a deadly disease.

It is this kind of fatalistic attitude that reinforces the sense of inferiority. We promise this outlook will sound foolish and shortsighted to you by the time you have completed this book!

CELEBRATE! ADHD

We plead for a revolutionary, yet commonsense attitude—one which acknowledges the difficulties, but celebrates the differences and advantages provided by ADHD. So let's put away the dour faces and fatalistic words.

Parents and teachers, reward these children for positives instead of simply punishing them for negatives. <u>Prevention is the best medicine</u>—proactively encouraging praise for positive behavior is far more effective (and enjoyable!) than reacting negatively.

Our kids like to be needed. They thrive on positive affirmation. You will be surprised how eager they are to please when you reward them for living up to higher expectations.

Let's celebrate their gifts, talents and passions with excitement…and show them the bright future that awaits them.

3: THE LITTLE TRAIN THAT COULDN'T

*We continually focus on what children with ADHD cannot do...
and then wonder why they are confused and directionless.*

Imagine if the little train from the fabled childhood story had ADHD.

Some therapists would have thoroughly conditioned the little train to believe it couldn't make it by focusing continually on all its weaknesses. Depleted of confidence, it would have never made it up over the hill. It may not have even tried.

But what qualities ultimately helped the little train succeed? Persistence and defiance in the face of struggle. An ability to hyperfocus and concentrate its energy on a large goal. A heart that responded to a big dream. The little train that could needed the very qualities that define children with ADHD.

BUT DON'T DEFICIENCIES REPRESENT REAL OBSTACLES?

"Okay," you say, "maybe we shouldn't focus only on what they cannot do. But these differences are really deficiencies."

Again, you get no argument from us. As an adult with ADHD, I have many, many deficiencies. I have difficulty beginning projects, processing verbal instructions and completing tasks which require sustained focus. Unless I'm interested in the task!

But keep in mind two important points:

1. Everyone has deficiencies to overcome, not only people with ADHD.
2. Successful people accentuate their strengths, not their weaknesses.

EVERYONE HAS DEFICIENCIES TO VERCOME

I have a friend who can speed read and comprehend everything in a flash. He has instant recall, a quick wit and a fast mind. He can devastate an opponent in a debate because of his ability to think on his feet. He understands processes and details, and has enormous patience. His world moves very slowly and deliberately. In other words, he is the exact opposite of me.

How does he do in the real world? Very well. Like school, most jobs are designed for people like him. Bright, reasoned, patient, able to connect the dots and follow established protocols.

He is everything we want our children to be, right? Listen to educators, therapists and doctors. 95% of their time is spent trying to change our children into people like my friend.

In reality, isn't that true? Isn't that the subtext of what we're ultimately trying to do? The medication, the constant focus on fixing what we think is wrong, the endless diagnoses...all are designed to change our children.

Our intentions are good—we want our children to have successful careers and families. We've been lead to believe that children like my friend grow into more "respectable" adults— the compliant, polite ones who don't ruffle any feathers.

But people like my friend have their issues:

- They never challenge the status quo and do something truly unique. They execute the mundane with supreme excellence and efficiency.

- Because they are not persistent and resilient, they shy away from challenging ventures. They sit on the sidelines and watch as the trailblazers develop creative products, change society and entertain us.

- More "stable" people like my friend tend to stay in comfortable routines, which breeds apathy.

- Because they are bright with quick minds, they can be arrogant and cutting.

- They often trust in their own intelligence and don't rely on others.

- Process-oriented, methodical people can be boring. Some of you may be pleading for a day of normalcy, but it's not all it's cracked up to be!

Ignoring equally debilitating character flaws that derail careers and relationships would be a huge mistake. Many struggle with being lazy, dishonest, bitter, arrogant, selfish or short-sighted.

Everyone has deficiencies.

THE SECRET TO WINNING THE SUPER BOWL

What separates overcomers and champions from the rest? They focus on their strengths and talents instead of their deficiencies.

It is a cold, snowy day at Foxboro Stadium south of Boston. Coach Bill Belichick is watching one of his rugged players struggle to kick field goals through the uprights. The coach sighs, rubs his hands over his face and wonders how he's going to win this critical playoff game.

"What's the matter with your foot, son?"

"Geez, Coach, I'm really working on it."

"Not good enough. You've gotta kick that ball through the uprights, you know."

"I can't do it right."

The coach shakes his head. This guy is his best athlete, a team leader, someone who can rally teammates with his charisma. But he's slow, can't kick, doesn't know how to block and isn't big enough to play defense.

"I've been practicing. Sometimes I can kick it far enough, but it's wide. Other times, I kick it straight, but it only goes ten yards."

"So what are we going to do?" Coach Belichick asks.

The player picks up the ball and throws a tight spiral, like a rocket. "Nice pass, Brady!" the receiver yells.

Tom Brady happens to be a certain Hall of Fame quarterback who has won three Super Bowl championships for the vaunted New England Patriots. He's known for his inspiring leadership, accurate throws and grace under pressure. But Coach Belichick is right—he is slow, can't kick a football and isn't big enough to play defense.

Wouldn't it be absurd if Coach Belichick spent all his time focusing on Tom Brady's inability to kick a football, run fast or play defense? Of course it would.

So why do we do the same thing to our kids?

STRAIGHT TALK

The lesson is clear: we need to focus on what our children can do, not what they cannot do.

Optimal performance in any venture is achieved by capitalizing on each person's natural strengths. This strategy doesn't work only on sports teams—it works in corporations, charities, ministries, families, government and community.

Would any of us subject ourselves to a work environment in which our boss designed our jobs around our weaknesses?

We shouldn't wonder why our children lack self-confidence, purpose and joy when all they hear is a constant chorus of "you aren't good at that."

In developing your child's path forward, are you going to play to his strengths or his weaknesses?

4: IGNORING NATURAL GIFTS AND TALENTS

We ignore or dismiss their natural gifts and talents—because they don't fit our narrow definition of success—and wonder why they are apathetic.

Jennifer H. lives in a suburb outside the nation's capital.

Ask Jennifer's parents about her, and they will tell you that even though her grades are slightly above average, Jennifer needs a lot of help. She has been diagnosed with six different learning disorders and difficulties. She spends two hours with a learning specialist every Monday and Wednesday after school. On Tuesdays and Fridays, she attends special education classes. And on Thursday, a psychiatrist helps relieve Jennifer's anxiety. Her parents will recount the thousands of dollars they have spent having her tested. They will show you mounds of reports explaining with precision every academic weakness she has.

During our two-hour visit with the family, not once do Jennifer's parents mention her natural gifts, talents or passions. Is Jennifer anxious because her parents are obsessed with fixing every weakness?

Ask Jennifer about her passions and her eyes light up. She will tell you she loves to read. She will proudly show you several short stories she has written about slaves' experiences in the Underground Railroad—they are quite impressive.

What else do we discover? Her room is covered with medals won in swimming and tennis competitions. And she expresses compassion for children with physical disabilities.

Jennifer's parents became so consumed with "fixing what was wrong" that they ignored her natural abilities. Refocusing their energies on developing Jennifer's gifts transformed their family.

NARROW DEFINITIONS OF SUCCESS

- How many of us push our kids to pursue a particular career path *we* have chosen?

- How many of us dissuade our kids from pursuing their passions because we don't think they can earn a good living?

- How many of us allow social status and prestige (attending a certain college or pursuing a particular profession) to take precedence over our child's fulfillment?

Success is developing and using our natural gifts, talents and passions to benefit others. These gifts and passions are inside for a reason.

ANOTHER CASUALTY: ATROPHY OF GIFTS

What happens when you don't use your muscles? They atrophy. The same thing happens to our children's gifts and talents.

Do you realize the absurdity of focusing exclusively on what our children cannot do rather than what they love doing? The time spent trying to fix weaknesses—and the resulting self-doubt—inhibits the development of their gifts. Soon they become walking wounded—unwilling or unable to express their talents because they've been surrounded by negativity and doubt for so long. The internal fire is extinguished.

Have you noticed how content and fulfilled your kids are when they are doing what they love? There is a reason why.

GIFTS AND PASSIONS CHANGE HISTORY

History would have been written differently had trailblazers focused on their weaknesses instead of pursuing their passions, often despite great adversity:

- Martin Luther King, Jr. would never have sacrificed his life to advance civil rights.

- Jonas Salk would never have pursued medicine and invented the polio vaccine.

- The Wright Brothers would have been accountants instead of pioneering flight.

- Mother Theresa would have pursued a career instead of becoming a champion of the poor and a role model for us all.

- Beethoven would have been a shopkeeper instead of a great composer. Stephen Spielberg would have been an engineer instead of an inspiring film-maker.

- Thomas Edison would have been an attorney instead of inventing practically every modern convenience we enjoy.

Our lives have been made richer by those who have pursued their gifts and passions instead of others' narrow definitions of success. Don't limit your child.

STRAIGHT TALK

Our children have gifts and talents for a reason. They are there to be used. When we ignore or place other things ahead of them, we devalue the gifts and an essential part of their being.

Their gifts and passions are part of who they are. It isn't surprising that when we begin to foster their gifts, talents and passions, they come alive with renewed confidence, purpose and joy. They begin to say, "I can" and see a larger purpose in life.

The resulting feelings of self-worth and competence extend into every area of life—including school and relationships.

Instead of wasting thousands of dollars and countless hours trying in vain to fix every weakness, let's invest that same energy and money into developing our child's gifts and passions.

5: DEMANDING SUCCESS IN EVERY SUBJECT

We demand success in every subject, even though schools exploit our children's weaknesses...and wonder why they are overwhelmed with anxiety.

UNREALISTIC STANDARDS

Sarah is an intensely curious ten-year-old living amidst the brick townhouses in colonial Virginia. She loves working with her hands—whether it is painting, sculpting or creating gingerbread houses—ice skating and performing in front of others. Sarah appears perfectly happy.

Despite her appetite for learning and enjoyment of reading, she has difficulty with short-term recall. She doesn't file information away efficiently. As a result, she doesn't test well, and her grades suffer.

Her parents are no different than most of us. They know Sarah is bright and they expect her to excel in every subject. After all, it just takes some extra work to move from C's to B's. And in order to qualify for a good prep school and college, Sarah needs a high G.P.A.

Her parents have made great sacrifices to pay for extensive testing...which shows that she isn't wired to do certain things well. She sees multiple learning specialists and therapists throughout the week.

Her father is an engineer who excels when solving complex problems, but possesses no skill in finance, marketing or sales. Sarah's mother is an accountant who can work wonders with numbers, but cannot think creatively. They have specialized in their industries to become experts in one subject.

They fail to discern the double standard.

SCHOOLS EXPLOIT THE WEAKNESSES OF CHILDREN WITH ADHD

While we expect and demand success from our kids (but not ourselves) in every subject, we subject them to a school system that exploits their weaknesses.

Our schools are purposefully structured in a way that plays to the strengths of kids who can sit, listen attentively and follow instructions; think in a linear manner and recall information quickly; and have a temperament for consistent, methodical work.

There is nothing wrong with this in an absolute sense, and it is not part of an evil plot to make life difficult for children with ADHD. It works perfectly for children who are wired to work in such a manner and provides profitable training for college and some careers.

But the opposite corollary remains true. Schools expose the weaknesses of children who are creative, entrepreneurial, prone to action more than listening; work in bursts of energy rather than methodically; and who tend to "graze" on information over time rather than recall it quickly.

Schools do not reward the use of skills and qualities with which children with ADHD are naturally wired.

WHO WILL HAVE DIFFICULTY IN SCHOOL?
Consider the following:

- A child who prefers experiential, hands-on learning (a classic doer) but has difficulty listening to a teacher for hours, will have difficulty in school.

- A child who has trouble sitting still in a chair for many hours a day will have difficulty in school.

- A child who likes to work independently and chart his own path, rather than follow instructions from a teacher, will have difficulty in school.

- A child who thinks creatively—daydreaming, pondering new ideas or writing stories in his head—rather than being organized and completing assignments quickly, will have difficulty in school.

- A child who works in short bursts of energy— finding inspiration and clarity throughout the day— rather than working consistently and methodically, will have difficulty in school.

Think about the qualities listed above: action-oriented, innovative, creative, independent learners. Are these inherently "bad" or "abnormal" qualities?

The answer is no.

But, these qualities can represent obstacles to success in school and some work environments.

WE CONDONE DOUBLE STANDARDS

Do we expect ourselves to be experts in every field or discipline at work? Absolutely not. We rely on highly specialized experts in finance, human resources, product development, research, marketing, manufacturing, technology, sales, accounting and various other departments. How would you feel if your boss expected you to excel in each of these different areas?

- Why is it okay for certain students to lack some attributes (e.g. creativity, risk-taking), but our kids are labeled as abnormal if they lack other attributes (e.g. quick processing and recall)?

- Why is it okay that some students are lost in unstructured environments that require independent work, but our kids are labeled if they don't thrive in structured classrooms?

- Why do we laugh when one student can only draw stick figures because he isn't "gifted" artistically, but we say something is wrong with our kids when they have difficulty working methodically?

- Why do we reward and praise kids who follow others and maintain the status quo, but label kids who are prone to action? Shouldn't we label the compliant ones with Energy Deficit Disorder?

CAPITALIZE ON STRENGTHS

Consider again the example of Christopher Campbell. Remember the classroom that he entered?

> The desks are not arranged in orderly rows. The lesson plan isn't written on the chalkboard. Canvasses, beanbag chairs and laptops are scattered across the room. Some kids are painting, some writing and still others building elaborate airplane models. The room is open and uncluttered, with plenty of sunlight and brightly colored walls. His classmates are working independently on their own projects.

Imagine the confidence and energy *this* classroom would engender in children with ADHD. It would capitalize on their natural wiring and accentuate their strengths.

Poor Christopher Campbell must have thought he had walked into a nightmare. The unstructured classroom requiring independent, creative work would have exposed his natural weaknesses.

Christopher Campbell's parents would call it unfair and demand that the school change his class.

Because Christopher couldn't produce brilliant portraits or write creative stories, they wouldn't say that he was being lazy, stupid or rebellious. They would say that he is different and that his teachers need to focus on his strengths.

And that's exactly what parents of children with ADHD should say.

STRAIGHT TALK

Children develop differently. Girls usually read earlier while boys excel in math at younger ages. Over time, they tend to catch up to each other. Don't be impatient if your child is struggling in a certain subject.

You are not an expert in every discipline at work. And your child is not going to excel in every subject.

Wouldn't you feel anxious if your boss quizzed you about disciplines at work about which you had no expertise? So how can you expect your child to struggle six hours a day, five days a week in school and still feel good about himself?

Encourage teachers to build lessons around your child's passions. Let your child read books that interest him. Is it really necessary for a fourth grade boy to read stories about Victorian-era girls? Or would it be fine if he read well-written stories about sports, airplanes or history?

Finally, realize that we need both generalists and specialists in life. For the most part, kids with ADHD hyperfocus on specific subjects or projects. This can be very beneficial. After all, if you needed brain surgery, would you request the brain surgeon or the family practitioner?

6 USING SCHOOL AS A PREDICTOR OF SUCCESS

We establish success in school as the predictor of success in life, judging our kids' performance against an artificial standard... and wonder why they have no hope.

ONE NAGGING CONCERN

If my child can't excel in school, how can he get into a good college? And how will he survive in the corporate world if he can't stay on task and complete projects?

We know the fear and apprehension in your voice. But we repeat this unequivocally: <u>performance in school is not a predictor of success in life.</u>

This thought is contrary to everything we have been taught. Learning is invaluable, but we challenge you to focus on what is truly important to achieve success in life.

SCHOOLS ARE AN ARTIFICIAL STANDARD

Schools are an artificial construct. Nothing in nature has ordained their current structure. For children with ADHD, maneuvering through school is similar to asking an infant to crawl through a maze—bruises, headaches and frustration guaranteed. Schools simply do not emphasize use of our kids' natural gifts and talents.

Therefore, assessing your child's future success using school as the metric merely consigns him to failure, you to disappointment and your family to unnecessary stress.

What if our schools were designed to meet the needs of creative kids with ADHD? Then who would have the problem sitting still, learning and completing assignments?

We do not excuse laziness or bad behavior. Neither should we confuse school with learning—they are not one and the same. School is one vehicle for learning, but not the only one.

OTHER WAYS TO LEARN

Think of the tremendous lessons your child learns at home and through involvement in extracurricular activities such as sports teams and Scouts. These are all valuable life skills necessary for a healthy and productive adult life:

> Leadership, teamwork, competition, commitment, discipline, motivation, overcoming adversity, building social relationships.

Hmmm. Sounds a lot like real life, huh?

Our kids are often curious about the stock market, our businesses, how to cook and the myriad decisions we make daily. Don't divide life into things adults do and things kids do.

Spend time taking care of everyday responsibilities with your child. Team him throughout the natural course of life.

SCHOOLS REINFORCE ARCANE SKILLS

The indispensable hallmarks of education are curiosity, the ability to think and the wisdom to apply knowledge to life situations. But in this age of enlightenment and scientific advancement, it is amazing how short-sighted we are in our view of what constitutes learning.

Consider the traits that are most important for success in traditional schools:
- Sit attentively at a desk
- Listen to a teacher lecture for hours
- Memorize facts and information
- Recall information for tests

How many times since completing your formal education have you been required to sit at a desk, listen to someone speak for hours, then memorize the information and be tested on your recall?

COMPARE SCHOOL TO REAL LIFE

Now compare the skills required for success in life with the skills required for success in school. You may find the exercise enlightening, even shocking.

List the qualities, skills and attributes necessary to forge success in your profession and develop meaningful relationships. Your list may look something like this:

> Hard work, leadership, teamwork, knowledge, intelligence, passion, drive, perseverance, discipline, problem-solving, creativity, integrity, ability to overcome obstacles, trust, love, compassion.

Now, let's make a list of the qualities that contribute to success in traditional schools:

> Attentiveness, compliance, recall, hard work, memorization, processing information quickly, testing well, working methodically.

How do the skills necessary for success in school compare to the qualities necessary for success in life? Of course there is some overlap. Children do learn valuable skills in school that will help them in the real world.

LIMITATIONS OF SCHOOL SKILLS

But in no way do children learn even the most valuable skills in school.

- Consider the most important qualities that set successful people apart. Aren't they usually intangibles like passion, drive, work ethic and integrity?

- Does success at work require good recall and testing skills, or the ability to access, analyze and apply information to specific situations?

- How many people graduate—even with advanced degrees–without a basic understanding of life skills? Do schools teach our children the principles necessary for healthy relationships, sound personal finance, entrepreneurship or career advancement?

COMPARE TRAITS OF ADHD WITH REAL LIFE—NOW WHO HAS THE ADVANTAGE?

Let's make a list of some common gifts, skills and traits shared by children with ADHD:

> Innovators who are energized by ideas; dreamers who are passionate about working toward a larger purpose and higher meaning; creative, intuitive feelers who are empathetic, sense others' emotions and spot trends; doers with boundless energy who prefer hands-on application and thrive on results, not process; persistent, defiant, resilient risk-takers unafraid to challenge the norm; independent workers able to hyperfocus and work in bursts of energy.

Now compare this list with the skills required for success in life. Hmmm. There is meaningful overlap. It is clear that success in the real world does not belong exclusively to those who are wired to achieve in school.

In fact, if you think about qualities required for success in certain professions—entrepreneurs, innovators, performing artists and leaders in every field—you can make a compelling argument that people with ADHD have a distinct advantage.

CONSIDER THE 7 HABITS

In case you still aren't convinced that children with ADHD possess qualities required for success in life even though they may struggle in school, consider Steven Covey's "7 Habits of Highly Effective People." Millions agree with Covey's pioneering research that these seven habits are critical in forging meaningful personal and professional relationships.

1. Be Proactive—be action-oriented in making changes.

2. Begin with the End in Mind—work toward a larger purpose.

3. Put First Things First—prioritize what is important.

4. Think Win/Win—seek mutually beneficial relationships.

5. Seek First To Understand, Then To Be Understood— practice empathy and selflessness.

6. Synergize—use mutual trust and understanding to solve conflict.

7. Sharpen the Saw—seek renewal physically, emotionally and spiritually.

I hope the point is obvious. None of these habits have anything to do with sitting attentively and passively acquiring knowledge. Children with ADHD often are naturally proactive, empathetic, intuitive and seek a larger purpose. Note how these qualities relate favorably to the 7 Habits. And do not forget that character—even more than knowledge—plays a distinct role in your child's success as an adult.

PRESSURE FROM SCHOOL IS DESTRUCTIVE

"When my son is away with me on business trips, he is bright, insightful and funny. I can see him being successful owning his own business. But school robs him of his self-confidence. I know that if I can get my son through school, he's going to thrive as an adult when he can pursue his passions.
--Michael F.

"My daughter came home from school like a zombie everyday. Her smile and curiosity were gone. When I mentioned homework, I saw the despair wash over her. But I noticed something during Christmas vacation. All of a sudden, I had my little girl back. Smiling, full of energy and ideas, singing and playing. I just didn't want to lose her again."
--Kristine P.

Using success in school as a predictor of success in life compounds the enormous pressure placed on children by teachers and parents—the important influencers in a child's life. Holding children with ADHD to unrealistic expectations in school can destroy their confidence and purpose.

During years that should be spent encouraging curiosity and feeding passions inside our children, we instead try to change their nature and force them to conform to a false standard.

We judge them against this standard five days a week, week in and week out, for nine months out of the year, for twelve years during their most formative years. The repeated, daily struggle and frustration eventually turns to anger, bitterness and apathy.

A relentlessly negative focus on a child's weaknesses can turn a hopeful child into a self-doubting skeptic. The feeling that every adult is against him leaves no safe place. School represents his failure. At home, the child and parents are thrust into an unending cycle of disappointments, stress and exhaustion. Fights over incomplete projects extend the nightmare into the evening and weekends.

Soon there is no time to relax, play and be a child.

STRAIGHT TALK

You must be willing to challenge the system—and your own preconceived ideas—to do what is best for your child. Not what is best for someone else's child. Not what is best for your reputation and social standing.

Do not allow artificial pressure to stifle your child's curiosity and creativity. And do not allow your apprehension and nervousness to douse their optimism in life.

Understand that success in life is not predicated on success in school. School is only one avenue for learning life skills. Success in school is not the goal—success in life is.

Take time now to celebrate the amazing qualities inside your child. Do you recognize qualities that could lead to success in many vocations? If that is the way your child is wired, shouldn't you be preparing him for that course in life?

7: FIGHTING THEIR OWN NATURE

We ask our kids to fight their own nature, to do things they cannot do no matter how hard they try...and wonder why they are frustrated and angry.

SQUANDERING A MILLION DOLLARS

If you offered me $1 million to assemble a car engine and gave me detailed instructions with the help of Dale Earnhardt, Jr.'s crew, I would trudge away empty-handed. You would hear me throwing wrenches before collapsing in frustration.

Ask me to sense what a stranger near me is feeling inside, and I can be psychic. But give me pages of instructions and something to assemble, and I don't know where to begin.

The bottom line is that you are asking me to do something I simply cannot do. It is not in my genetic wiring. In third grade, tests showed I was deficient in spatial relations. Fortunately, my parents did not overreact and insist that I take special classes to overcome this weakness. It wouldn't have helped.

Trying to correct all of our kids' natural weaknesses can cause extreme frustration. Imagine if my parents had sent me to a special after-school class to learn how to assemble models. I would have spent hours fighting my own nature. Ultimately, it would have destroyed my self-confidence.

Just as important, it would have also robbed me of positive experiences playing sports and developing my gifts and passions.

COMPETING ON THE WRONG PLAYING FIELD

We are asking children with ADHD to compete on a playing field that is often hostile to their strengths and natural wiring.

Let's say we put Michael Jordan, the greatest basketball player ever, on a soccer field. He's a tremendous athlete, right? A leader, a champion. But if you force him to use his feet instead of his hands on a field of grass, he suddenly becomes mediocre.

Imagine if your boss asked you to do something at work that you simply could not do. How would you feel?

We send our children to compete on a playing field in which success is based on exercising their weaknesses, not their strengths. It's like asking your right-handed child to bat left-handed, then badgering him from the bleachers because he can't hit.

We don't demand this from ourselves at work, nor do we expect it from highly trained athletes. If Michael Jordan cannot compete on a different playing field, then why do we expect children with ADHD to thrive in an environment that does not favor their strengths?

Each person's brain is wired to do certain tasks, but not wired to do others. It is no different than asking someone who isn't wired creatively to paint a landscape or write a song. They could spend weeks trying, but never really get it. Because they aren't wired that way.

Fighting nature is always dangerous and ineffective.

STRAIGHT TALK

Parents, you can try to turn your child into whatever you want them to be. In the end, you will lose and nature will win.

Fighting your child's nature only leads to frustration, resentment, anger and disillusionment. And these emotional problems lead to far more debilitating issues than the ADHD itself.

You must face the fact that there are some things your child will never be good at. Period.

Each person is born with a genetic predisposition toward certain skills and talents.

We have a simple choice to make: are we going to work with our child's natural wiring or against it?

8: CHANGING OUR CHILD, INSTEAD OF CHANGING OURSELVES

We try to change our children—through pressure and medication—instead of changing the way we teach or view them...and wonder why they lack a strong identity.

FORCING A SQUARE PEG INTO A ROUND HOLE

In our enlightened age which despises mass commercialization—and in which customization for individual needs is a prerequisite for success—we still teach all children the same way. And we still maintain the same expectations for each child regardless of wiring.

Despite advances in understanding how the human brain works, we have not adapted and applied these learnings to most schools. We are stuck in a 1908 paradigm that resembles Henry Ford's automobile production line. *Yes, you can have any car you want, as long as it's a black Model-T.*

Ample evidence makes it clear that children have different learning styles. Yet, we make every child learn the same way.

Rather than change the way we teach kids with ADHD, we try to *change our kids* and their natural wiring. We are, in essence, trying to squeeze a square peg into a round hole.

And the results are obvious.

CHANGING NATURE THROUGH SUFFOCATING EXPECTATIONS

How many of us want the compliant, adorable child with the manners of Wally Cleaver and maturity to speak well with adults? The kind of child we can show off at the office to the adulation of our colleagues? The child who naturally excels in school and asks for advanced placement classes? The kind of child who grows up to become a respected professional—an executive, a doctor, an engineer.

You get the picture. If we are honest, many of us will admit with shame that we have this image and desire in our hearts. But we must realize that our expectations only complicate our child's life.

And ultimately yield the opposite effect we are striving to achieve.

CHANGING NATURE THROUGH MEDICATION

Given that virtually every human weakness or shortcoming has been labeled a disorder or dysfunction of one kind or another, it is no surprise that corresponding prescription medications have been developed.

Kids today are inundated with too much sugar, too much television and too much medication.

We should be alarmed that of every 100 kids who walk into a psychiatrist's office with the symptoms of ADHD, 75 will walk out—after their very first visit—with a prescription in hand for a stimulant drug.

WHY ARE WE MEDICATING?

Medication should not be given to make life more convenient for ADULTS!

- Are we medicating our difficult child to make him compliant and act like everyone else?

- Are we medicating our child so that the resulting lack of energy will help him behave better in school and at home?

- Are we, therefore, medicating our child for our own convenience as parents and teachers?

- Are we medicating our child because we have determined that he cannot succeed in school without medication?

- Why is medicating our <u>first</u> option and not our last?

- Why do we expect a ten-year-old to bear all the responsibilities for changing? Shouldn't adults be responsible first?

Heart patients must take medication to regulate their blood flow. They do not have another option. Children with infections must take antibiotics. They do not have another option.

Our kids have other options. We must pursue alternatives first.

DANGERS OF MEDICATION

In addition to the physical risks and documented side-effects of prescription drugs (which should not be minimized), the gravest danger is to our child's self-worth and sense of identity.

When we seek to change our children by using medication, we send the following insidious messages:

- There is something wrong with who you are.

- You are inferior.

- Your energy and creativity are bad and must be diminished or eliminated.

- You must change your nature to be successful.

- You are not capable of self-control without the help of a pill.

- You are powerless and therefore not responsible for your own actions.

What is the impact on a child's confidence, identity and self-worth when authority figures insist he needs to be someone else, and that a pill is necessary for him to succeed?

SHOULD WE MEDICATE?

By now, our answer should not surprise you.

Your attitude toward ADHD is more potent than any medicine.

We must *change the child's environment and expectations first* before changing his nature through medication. Medicating children should only be a last resort.

In fact, prevention is the best medicine. Many of the behavioral issues we seek to modify with medication can be prevented by first praising children for their good behavior and positive choices. When we wait for our children to misbehave, and then devote our energy to yelling and enforcing rules, we simply encourage more bad behavior.

Instead, we need to proactively use our energy to encourage and praise them for desired actions (thereby naturally discouraging negative behaviors and reactions).

Parents and teachers must modify their expectations, learn to accentuate each child's strengths and reduce stressors. Don't keep the environment the same and expect a medication to change everything.

Teachers must adapt their teaching styles to help visual and experiential learners. Allow kids to read books and magazines that interest them. Draw out their gifts and passions.

STRAIGHT TALK

Change your child's environment. Change his diet. Change your expectations. Change your teaching style. But let's stop trying to change our children.

Teachers who want to temper children's intensity and creativity are unwittingly robbing themselves of perhaps their most curious and interesting students. These are kids with active minds. They need to be engaged more effectively by incorporating their passions and gifts into lesson plans.

Parents, work to eliminate your child's dependence on medication. Teach him self-awareness and demonstrate practical ways to respond to situations differently. Transform your home into a safe haven filled with praise and encouragement. Better nutrition—through commonsense changes such as eating more fruits, nuts and vegetables and reducing consumption of sugar and processed foods—helps improve mental sharpness and memory while reducing anxiety.

Change commitments and provide flexibility in your schedule to reduce external stressors. Expose your child to activities he naturally enjoys doing. Consider home schooling.

We should always believe in the better angels of our child's nature, not the worst.

We should never send the message that our child can be successful only if we change who he is.

9: TRUSTING EXPERTS RATHER THAN PARENTS

We cede care of our children to "experts" with an endless chorus of diagnoses rather than trusting our own instincts as parents...and wonder why our kids no longer respond to us.

There are countless teachers, therapists, educators, psychologists and psychiatrists who do amazing work with children every day. In no way do we intend to minimize their hard work, dedication and care for children.

But parents must not relinquish primary care for their kids to professionals simply because they have a certain title or level of education. Many parents betray their own instincts because they are intimidated by "the professionals." *Who am I to know what is best when these experts have advanced degrees?*

Many of the experts are flat out wrong about kids with ADHD. They have prescribed elaborate tests, rigorous treatment and medication that are not always warranted. They have assigned labels and said "there is something wrong" with children with ADHD who have "abnormal" brains.

We have coached kids diagnosed with several different disorders, who really had one or two major weaknesses that should have been overshadowed by their many gifts.

Consider the following:

- Most professionals are trained to find problems. Their vocation is "fixing what is wrong."

- A reading specialist may uncover a spelling problem. But absent an understanding that the child may have ten other strengths—among them language and grammar—the specialist will recommend treatment for one specific weakness.

- "Success" for "experts" is completely dependent upon academic achievement. They must earn advanced degrees, so excelling at memorization and recall is paramount to them. School is all they know. Most have not worked in "the real world."

- The ones who define what is "normal" and "abnormal" are biased by their own wiring, which may be completely opposite of our kids'. It doesn't fit *their own* preconceived ideas of what is normal.

- A teacher trying to manage two dozen kids may do what is most expedient to reduce her stress and keep class moving along, whether it is recommending medication or teaching each child the same way.

- Doctors, psychologists and learning specialists sometimes get comfortable making the same diagnosis for each child who fits a certain pattern. Seek them out, listen to them, but do not take their advice as the final word.

We applaud teachers who adapt their teaching styles for children with ADHD by using visual and experiential learning tools, involving kids in class and focusing on their gifts.

Unfortunately, we have heard numerous firsthand accounts of educators who have given up on our kids and uttered damaging remarks such as, "I don't know what can be done with that scattered brain of yours."

We must be our child's fiercest advocate.

A DISTURBING THOUGHT

Nothing is more disturbing than a quote posted on a popular website that purports to encourage people with ADHD:

> Scientists are studying causes in an effort to identify better ways to treat, and someday, to prevent ADHD.

The fact that a leading advocacy group views ADHD as a disease to be prevented and eradicated is chilling. Unfortunately, too many professionals believe that ADHD is a dreadful condition that dooms kids to failure.

If ADHD were eradicated, society would suffer the loss of the great passion, depth and creativity provided by people wired so uniquely.

Why would we want everyone to think the same way? Why won't researchers invest their time discovering the many ways ADHD is advantageous?

STRAIGHT TALK

Parents, you know inside what is best for your child. You have birthed, raised and taught your child most of what he or she knows. You have worked in the real world and seen the qualities essential for success.

Trust your own instincts.

10: FEEDING CHILDREN A DIET OF SCORN

We feed our children a diet of scorn and disapproval...and wonder why they seek positive affirmation and belonging from other disaffected kids.

We are universally horrified when we see stories of children who have been deprived of proper care and nutrition, fed a diet of nothing more than sugar and processed foods. We rightly shudder at the thought of their health.

But we do the same thing to our children mentally, emotionally and spiritually. We feed them a constant diet of scorn and disapproval from a young age—there is something wrong with them, they are lazy and incapable, they are failures.

What is the normal reaction for someone who has felt acutely the subtle looks of disdain from his parents, the scornful eyes of his teachers and the frustrated glances of psychologists?

Our children will seek affirmation and a sense of belonging from someone. And if we don't provide it, they will find it among other disaffected kids who share their pain and rejection, kids who can relate to the negativity and labels.

Many turn to risky behaviors such as drug or alcohol abuse to escape the oppressive environment. The danger is exacerbated because kids with ADHD can be genetically predisposed to seek risky behavior.

CONCLUSION

While the symptoms caused directly by ADHD—distractibility and inattention, impulsivity and hyperactivity—provide their share of challenges, our attitude toward children with ADHD causes more problematic issues:

> Lack of confidence, low self-worth and poor identity; frustration, anger and disillusionment; anxiety, stress and depression; guilt and self-blame; lack of direction; conflict in relationships.

One of the great tragedies is the opportunity cost to society. All of the time spent fighting our child's nature—instead of developing, nurturing and optimizing it—forces us to squander an entire generation's gifts, talents and passions.

Were we to embrace and work with our child's natural wiring, we would unleash a wave of creativity and innovation that could transform society. Read on to see how we can do this!

THE MOST IMPORTANT QUESTION

No matter how frustrated you become, no matter how dire the situation seems, no matter how much your child struggles with school, you should keep one simple question top of mind.

How is my child's heart?

Tack this question onto your refrigerator, your computer screen and your heart. Sure, your child may be struggling with school and relationships. But how is her heart? Is she kind and giving and compassionate? Does she forgive others and ask for forgiveness for her own shortcomings?

Does your son show courage, fortitude and resolve when challenges arise? Does your daughter have insight into people and an ability to inspire others? Does your son have compassion for others or show sparks of creativity that amaze you?

Our society places too much importance on the mind. Your child is not the sum of his experience in school or strength of his executive function. The mind is only one component of a person that influences his success in life. Consider the most impressive people in society—they are people whose courage, leadership and vision have transformed the world.

Our son has his struggles. But when we lay our heads on our pillows at night and consider the larger picture, we are always reassured by the most important thought—our son has a really good heart.

III.

Ten Reasons We Celebrate!ADHD

10 REASONS WE CELEBRATE!ADHD

We Celebrate Children With ADHD Because...

1. They are purposefully wired differently, not deficiently.

2. They are the next generation of trailblazing innovators, entrepreneurs, artists, musicians, inventors and leaders.

3. They possess advantageous traits that enrich society.

4. They are positioned to thrive in a future defined by self-directed entrepreneurship and risk-taking.

5. The attributes most consider negative are actually positive when applied constructively.

6. Developing their gifts, talents and passions restores confidence, purpose and joy.

7. They are idealistic, world-changers whose larger vision helps curb short-term, impulsive behavior.

8. They have giving hearts with a need to find purpose.

9. They possess the fortitude and persistence to overcome obstacles.

10. They are content inside and possess the compassion and intuition necessary to forge intimate relationships.

CREATE AN ACTION PLAN

In order to achieve the greatest transformation within your family, it is critical that you actively participate in creating an Action Plan for you and your child.

Place the book down for a moment and grab a notebook or pad of paper to keep by your side. Now let's begin the transformation!

1 THINK DIFFERENT, WONDERFULLY DIFFERENT

We celebrate children with ADHD because they are purposefully wired differently, not deficiently.

Your child is not a mistake. He needs to know that. And you need to realize that as well.

Your child needs to believe deep inside that he is genetically designed the way he is meant to be. His design is a good design, and he has a higher purpose.

The purpose of our organization is to help children celebrate their unique wiring. Your child needs to like himself. He needs to appreciate his differences and see that they are good!

Before your child can have healthy relationships with others, he must first have a healthy relationship with himself. How can he expect others to like and respect him if he doesn't like himself?

We know that we have succeeded when the kids we Coach or have at Trailblazers Camp say, "I really like who I am."

Our job as parents is to instill this self-worth in our children and help them use their natural gifts and passions to fulfill their purpose.

This is the first step in celebrating ADHD!

DIFFERENCES ARE NECESSARY

By now, you can see how people's gifts and talents work together in unison. Do you recognize the wonderful symmetry?

Consider how our economy thrives. Through insight into people and trends, an entrepreneur develops a creative solution to a consumer need. Many people have ideas, but only those who have the energy, focus and temperament to take risks make it happen. Entrepreneurs start businesses from nothing more than an idea and create a functioning enterprise.

In order to make the business efficient and expand profitably, there is a need for structure and processes. And who is best suited for that task? People who think methodically, are risk-averse and thrive at organizing become the company's managers.

Do you see that there are some people who are naturally gifted at generating new ideas and starting ventures while others are more gifted at managing the business? Do you see how school prepares people well for general management positions while real life experiences form the foundation for entrepreneurs?

Our brains are wired specifically to optimize certain traits, not all of them. If I spent my energy trying to remember details and manage processes, it would crowd out and confuse the part of my brain that generates ideas and creative solutions.

"He couldn't see the forest for the trees." That is by design. We need people who can see the forest, and we also need those who know each individual tree by name.

How is your child wired?

DEFINE CHILDREN BY THEIR STRENGTHS, NOT WEAKNESSES

We must not allow our children to be defined by ADHD or their weaknesses. Can you imagine these famous people being identified by what they <u>cannot do</u> instead of what they can?

> Would Bill Gates introduce himself as a lousy painter, or as the entrepreneurial founder of Microsoft?

> Would you invite Emeril Lagasse to your house to fix your car, or to cook an unbelievable meal?

> Would baseball player Roger Clemens be introduced as a terrible batter or a Hall-of-Fame caliber pitcher?

This seems ridiculous, doesn't it? But how often do we refer to our children by their weaknesses? This focus on the negativity of ADHD can become suffocating and self-fulfilling. Is it any wonder our kids suffer from anxiety and lack confidence?

Rather, our children should be defined by their gifts, talents and passions. They should be encouraged by their competitive advantages. They are creative innovators who see the big picture and develop breakthrough ideas. They use their intuition to spot consumer trends and are unafraid to try new ventures, with the steadfastness to overcome hardships.

This is a necessary foundation to helping our kids like themselves.

ACTION PLAN #1: THINK DIFFERENT, WONDERFULLY DIFFERENT

Make a list of 10 strengths or character traits that make your child wonderfully different (example below).

My son is wonderfully different because:

1.   He has a big heart and always wants to help others.

2.   He has his own unique style and is comfortable in his own skin.

3.   He has strong opinions and isn't afraid to stand up for himself.

4.   He has so much personality—he can be serene or animated, pensive or hilariously funny.

5.   He is entirely unpredictable—you never know what he is going to do.

6.   He's always figuring out ways to make things better.

7.   He has boundless curiosity.

8.   He has an unending supply of new ideas for businesses.

9.   He is tenacious when he believes in something. He will be a leader, not a follower.

10.   He makes wise decisions about relationships.

Now begin sharing with your child all the reasons you like who he is. Encourage his strengths and you will change his heart.

2 CELEBRATE YOUR TRAILBLAZER

We celebrate children with ADHD because they are the next generation of trailblazing innovators, entrepreneurs, artists, musicians, inventors and leaders.

7 QUALITIES OF EFFECTIVE TRAILBLAZERS

Did you know that the seeds of greatness necessary to be a trailblazer are the very qualities inside children with ADHD?

1. Innovators who are energized by ideas.

2. Dreamers who are passionate about pursuing a larger purpose and higher meaning.

3. Creative thinkers who see the world differently and develop solutions.

4. Intuitive feelers who are empathetic, sense others' emotions, spot consumer trends, and develop innovative products to meet emerging consumer needs.

5. Doers who are prone to action, work independently with boundless energy, prefer hands-on application and thrive on results, not processes.

6. Risk-takers unafraid to challenge the norm.

7. Persistent, defiant, resilient contrarians who don't give up when someone says, "You can't do it."

INSPIRATION: FAMOUS FACES OF ADHD

Have you ever been to DisneyWorld? Played Playstation2? Listened to your favorite music on an iPod? Watched a fighter jet soar overhead at Mach 3? Watched *Toy Story* or *Pirates of the Caribbean* in Dolby Sound?

What do all of these products and experiences have in common? They were designed or developed by trailblazers whose contributions to society are immeasurable...and who were wired to do so. They possessed the qualities most closely identified with ADHD. So did Monet, Beethoven and many others. Your child is in good company.

Children with ADHD should be very confident about their future. History is replete with examples of innovators, entrepreneurs, artists, musicians, inventors, revolutionaries and leaders in every field who shared the characteristics of ADHD.

As you read these profiles, identify the trailblazing qualities your child possesses.

TRAILBLAZING DIRECTOR

This boy's fascination with film was obvious from a young age. He charged admission to home movies featuring staged crashes of his Lionel trains. Before he was a teenager, he had written, directed and produced his first movie. At the age of sixteen, he earned $100 profit showing his first full-length film at a local movie theater.

His dreams appeared to be crushed when he was rejected by film school. But he would not be deterred. During a tour of Universal Studios in Hollywood, he jumped off the bus and explored the back lots. He converted an abandoned janitor's closet into a makeshift office. Soon security guards were waving the young man in a Bar Mitzvah suit through the gates.

And the rest is history. Most directors would consider their career a success with even one of these films to their credit. The following innovative, blockbuster movies are only a sampling of the work of trailblazer Steven Spielberg:

Jaws, Close Encounters of the Third Kind, Raiders of the Lost Ark, E.T. the Extra-Terrestrial, Indiana Jones and the Temple of Doom, The Color Purple, Jurassic Park, Schindler's List and Saving Private Ryan.

TRAILBLAZING DREAMER

This young boy learned to escape his father's cruelty by drawing. After leaving home at 16 to join the Red Cross Ambulance Corps during World War II, he discovered that he could create his own little world with animated cartoons. While he possessed incredible creativity, he lacked business sense. Many of his ideas were stolen from him.

Tired of living life as a true starving artist, he moved to Los Angeles to partner with his older brother, a savvy businessman. Free to focus on his creative pursuits, he became the first to add music and sound effects to a cartoon.

He later took a huge risk and built what many warned would be a massive failure. He didn't listen to the doubters. You and your children have probably been enthralled as you've strolled through his Magic Kingdom. Generations of children have grown up loving Mickey Mouse. And how many Walt Disney movies have captured the innocence and idealism of family life that eluded him?

Not bad for a man who was once fired by a newspaper editor who claimed he had "no good ideas."

TRAILBLAZING SCIENTIST

This trailblazing scientist was unique because he relied on intuition as a researcher. He sensed and believed that spiritual values transcended science. His work was motivated by working toward a larger purpose to benefit others.

He was a mediocre chemistry student in college. But his discovery that most infectious diseases are caused by germs became the foundation for the science of microbiology, and a cornerstone of modern medicine.

He advocated changes in hospital practices to minimize the spread of disease by microbes. He discovered that weakened forms of a microbe could be used as an immunization against more virulent forms of the microbe. Because he didn't rely merely on what could be "seen" by the physical world, he revealed the world of viruses so small they couldn't be seen under a microscope.

As a result, he developed techniques to vaccinate dogs against rabies, and to treat humans bitten by rabid dogs.

If you've ever enjoyed a glass of cold milk with hot chocolate chip cookies, you can thank this man. He developed the process by which harmful microbes are destroyed using heat, without destroying the food. The process is called pasteurization. And his name is Louis Pasteur.

TRAILBLAZING INVENTOR

He had an unusually broad forehead and large head. He did not learn to speak until he was almost four years old. His teacher believed that his brains were scrambled, so his mother home schooled him.

He rejected formal learning and satisfied his boundless curiosity through self-instructed reading, experimentation and examination. He compensated for shortcomings in unique ways. He was mostly deaf, but turned this obstacle into an advantage by tuning out the noisy world to stay more focused.

Throughout his teen years, he started numerous businesses that ultimately helped fund a chemical laboratory in his basement. Later he would establish the largest and most influential scientific laboratory in the world.

Before that moment came, however, he would struggle. He was deeply in debt and once begged for tea on the streets. Western Union almost fired him for excessive moonlighting and not concentrating on his primary responsibilities.

Ultimately, his tinkering and moonlighting paid off. Consider the following sample of his many achievements:

- At 29, he almost beat Alexander Graham Bell to the punch in inventing the telephone.
- He invented the phonograph.
- He invented the incandescent electric light bulb.
- He introduced the world's first economically viable system of centrally generating and distributing electric light, heat, and power.
- He invented the first practical dictaphone, mimeograph, and storage battery.
- He created the first silent film and then added audio to moving images to produce talking pictures.

Though he was internationally revered and a major stockholder in the General Electric Corporation (which grew out of his efforts), he had only a few close friends.

At the age of 83, he obtained his final (1,093rd) patent. Despite his "scrambled brains," lack of formal education and learning and speech difficulties, Thomas Edison has been hailed by many as the greatest inventor of all time...and a man who shaped modern civilization more than any other man since Gutenberg.

TRAILBLAZING ARTIST

He was unpredictable and inconsistent, and never showed interest in school. His family relationships were strained. He became a loner obsessed with work and controlling everything in his life. Loss of control caused him great frustration. He was able to hyperfocus on projects. Sound familiar?

If you've ever been to Rome, you've probably seen his enduring work adorning the Sistine Chapel. The great 16th century artist Michelangelo may have suffered from symptoms of ADHD or high-functioning autism.

He was able to generate, in a short time, hundreds of sketches for the Sistine ceiling—each unique with different poses. He gave his undivided attention to his masterpieces. And millions are thankful for his dedication.

TRAILBLAZING AIRLINE ENTREPRENEUR

This innovator learned about customer service working in his grandfather's convenience store as a young boy.

After dropping out of college, he started a travel agency, a charter service and low-cost airline. Southwest Airlines bought his fledgling airline, but fired him after only five months because his animated management style ruffled too many feathers.

A few years later, he founded JetBlue Airlines and pioneered many bold innovations—including e-ticketing, automatic ticket machines, and at-home reservation staffs. His intuition and focus on listening to customers provided a competitive advantage against the bigger airlines.

Today, JetBlue CEO David Neeleman enthusiastically credits ADHD with sparking his innovative ideas and insight into consumer trends.

TRAILBLAZING REVOLUTIONARIES

Every year on the 4th of July, Americans proudly celebrate their independence with fireworks and parades. But without patriots whose strong sense of internal justice and willingness to challenge authority enabled them to put their highest ideals above their own safety, we would never have had the courage to declare our independence as a nation.

These are traits of people with ADHD. These are qualities that animated revolutionary patriots like Samuel Adams and Patrick Henry.

No doubt they were not the easiest men to live with while inciting a revolution—can you imagine Mrs. Henry's reaction to her husband's famous battlecry, "Give me liberty or give me death!"—but their commitment and trailblazing attitudes helped forge a new nation.

TRAILBLAZING ARTISTS AND MUSICIANS

Some common traits run through the lives of artists and musicians whose work we celebrate centuries after their deaths. Men such as Beethoven, Monet and Picasso were never understood or appreciated in their own lifetimes. They exhibited quirky behavior.

But they saw and heard the world in different ways, and captured their innovative interpretations on canvas and paper. And the world has been made richer because of them.

ACTION PLAN # 2: CELEBRATE YOUR TRAILBLAZER

Make a list of your child's trailblazing qualities. Take some time to think how you can channel those qualities into healthy, positive pursuits and passions.

3 CELEBRATE COMPETITIVE ADVANTAGES

We celebrate children with ADHD because they possess advantageous, superior traits that enrich society.

TAKE STOCK OF COMPETITIVE ADVANTAGES

Current research strives to understand the *disadvantages* caused by ADHD. But we challenge the medical community to seek to understand the *unique advantages and gifts* children with ADHD possess that are essential for a thriving society.

Do we actually believe that rather than being inferior, children with ADHD possess skills and character traits superior to their peers? Absolutely.

We will demonstrate in this chapter how people with ADHD have superior wiring in specific situations, and how these differences uniquely benefit society. In the following chapter, we will show why people with ADHD are uniquely positioned to capitalize on future societal trends.

SUPERIOR WIRING

Instead of focusing on the negative and trying to merely minimize our weaknesses, we need to proactively help our children turn their unique qualities into competitive advantages.

> A company sees an immediate opportunity to penetrate a new market, but the path is uncertain. Do they turn to the risk-averse manager who thinks through tasks

methodically and follows established processes? Or do they turn to the action-oriented pioneer who works independently and busts down doors, whose ability to hyperfocus and place considerable energy on an important task is the key to success?
Advantage ADHD.

Show me someone who has the passion and empathy to help people, whose internal drive, energy and enthusiasm propel him to overcome obstacles…and I will show you the leader of a vibrant charity that is helping thousands of people.
Advantage ADHD.

Our world is filled with problems begging for solutions. Who is wired better to meet needs than someone who has insight into consumers, isn't afraid to try new things, has boundless energy and doesn't get deterred when others tell him it can't be done? This is the person with ADHD. This is the *Entrepreneur of the Year* candidate.
Advantage ADHD.

How many times have you ventured to a movie theater to escape to another world? How many times have you needed that stirring song to lift your spirits? Chances are that you were inspired by a writer, director, actor or musician who happens to be incredibly creative.
Advantage ADHD.

Okay, you get the point. There are limitless situations in which a person with the traits of ADHD has a competitive advantage.

GIFTS ENRICH SOCIETY

A world which has squandered the gifts of an entire generation desperately needs the positive contributions of children with ADHD.

- How many non-profit charities have been started by people with big hearts working to change lives?
- How many new products and businesses have been created to make our lives richer, more productive and easier?
- How many of the cool products and services most of us enjoy were created by people with ADHD?

Could that child who is struggling in school be the next Beethoven, Mark Twain, Monet or Bill Gates? Could that child obsessed with science develop a vaccine that saves millions of lives? Could that child who is always tinkering with mechanical operations develop a breakthrough hybrid vehicle that dramatically reduces pollution and dependence on fossil fuels?

What would America look like if we stifled everyone who has ADHD? There would be a huge outcry in our popular culture because the best movies, songs and products are created by people with the attributes of ADHD.

You may as well shut down Blockbuster and your local movie theater; Barnes & Noble and Borders; radio stations; Best Buy and Circuit City; music and video game stores; and the thousands of small businesses we count on daily for food and entertainment.

We need people with ADHD.

ACTION PLAN # 3: CELEBRATE COMPETITIVE ADVANTAGES

First, list the advantageous qualities and competitive advantages your child possesses.

Next, imagine different ways he can use his gifts to enrich society.

For many of you, your child's first school years have been consumed with negativity and an unrelenting focus on his weaknesses. These exercises are intended to provoke and inspire a transformation in the way you view and interact with your child. And in the way your child sees himself and his future.

4 CAPITALIZE ON FUTURE TRENDS

We celebrate children with ADHD because they are positioned to thrive in a future defined by self-directed entrepreneurship and risk-taking.

TRAILBLAZERS ARE TOMORROW'S LEADERS

The hierarchies that once dominated social institutions and corporations are being replaced by less centralized, more autonomous enterprises and individuals. Traditional corporate jobs are dwindling. Entrepreneurs creating small businesses now provide over 90% of new jobs.

A mere thirty years ago, most of the nation turned to three big networks for their news. Then pioneer Ted Turner founded CNN and turned the news world on its head with 24-hour cable coverage. Now informal networks of individual bloggers are using the internet to break news stories to meet the needs of the instant consumer.

While many of us grew up in an era in which wealth was created by executives managing large corporations, the future will provide increasing competitive advantage to businesses that uncover unmet consumer needs and respond quickly with meaningful products and services.

Who is best positioned for success in this future economy? Action-oriented individuals who have insight into consumer trends, thrive in self-directed enterprise, are unafraid to take risks, seize the momentum and hyperfocus to create new products and services.

While the managers in large corporations are still forming committees, commissioning studies, debating their options and pushing papers through the bureaucracy, entrepreneurs blessed with the attributes of ADHD are busy creating solutions.

It is no surprise that the fastest growing segment of our consulting services is helping companies create entrepreneurial cultures. We help identify and train leaders who can discover and capitalize on growth opportunities. And our best candidates always have ADHD!

OUR SKILLS ARE MORE UNIQUE
It is easier for those of us with ADHD to be analytical, master details and become more organized than for linear thinking people to be like us.

Think how difficult it is for a non-ADHD person to change his nature and suddenly become a risk-taker, idea generator or creative artist, writer or musician. Not easy at all.

This is a small point, but another reason to Celebrate!ADHD.

A RADICAL IDEA

We are proposing a radical idea that should be common sense. Let's stop trying to force our kids into the same bucket and assuming that there is only one path to success. We need to treat our children with respect as individuals and consider the path that is right for them.

We grew up in households that stressed the necessity of a college education, so it has been difficult to admit the following: a college education is not for everyone.

Think about the people you admire from history, as well as friends, colleagues and acquaintances you consider successful. Many of them did not achieve success in school or follow a path normally associated with success. Bill Gates never graduated from college. Richard Branson failed to complete high school. Yet you've seen in these people many amazing qualities that led to success.

We have begun charting a new course for the millions of children blessed with an entrepreneurial spirit or creative gift. They are not wired to thrive in traditional schools, so why not create an educational experience that fosters development of their natural gifts and passions?

We intend to open our first *School of Creativity and Entrepreneurship* in 2006. While traditional schools prepare kids for college, we want to prepare kids for life.

Let's help our children follow their unique wiring. If your child wants to go to college, do everything you can to help him get into the school that will prepare him best for his chosen field. But if you have a child who years to be an entrepreneur or a performing artist, why should you spend twelve years preparing him for an event that is not right for him?

Instead, we should invest our considerable resources to develop our child's passions.

Would a college education benefit our son? Of course it would. But we know that he is wired with the essential qualities of an entrepreneur with a passion for owning his own businesses. Should we force our son to be like everyone else, or should we develop a plan that capitalizes on his natural gifts and passions?

We have actively begun teaching our son how to be an entrepreneur. He is developing his own businesses at age 12 and learning the practical skills necessary for success in life.

We intend to follow the bold move of some friends in our community. Instead of investing a considerable sum to send their child to college for four years, they provided seed money to fund several entrepreneurial ventures.

By age 22, their son had started three businesses and gained four years of real world business experience. One business failed (a valuable experience!), but the other two ventures are now profitable and he is doing what he loves.

ACTION PLAN # 4: CAPITALIZE ON FUTURE TRENDS

Make a list of ways that your child can leverage his gifts, talents and passions to capitalize on future trends. How can you provide opportunities to learn how to be an entrepreneur or performing artist now?

5 TURN NEGATIVES INTO POSITIVES

We celebrate children with ADHD because the attributes most consider negative are actually positive when applied constructively.

CELEBRATE QUALITIES MOST CONSIDER NEGATIVE

Many of our kids' qualities are deemed negative because they inconvenience us or someone else—or because they contribute to difficulties in school.

Our greatest weaknesses are usually our greatest strengths, and our greatest strengths are our greatest weaknesses. Our job as parents is to evaluate these traits within a broader perspective and turn negative tendencies into positives.

ENERGIZED BY IDEAS

What parents haven't complained about their child consumed with ideas, ideas, ideas?

In our shortsightedness, we demand that our kids master the details and live life in regimented routines. While some are wired to manage enterprises and make sure the trains run on time, our kids develop the ideas that create better trains.

Ideas spawn the newest technologies, products and services society seeks. Who do you think developed the iPod, PlayStation and plasma televisions consumers crave?

And ideas change cultures. It was the liberating idea that a nation should be defined by self-government that led American patriots to overthrow the British crown. It was the emancipating idea that all men are created equal that led abolitionists to fight for the freedom of slaves. It was the idea that freedom is the right of every individual that caused the Berlin Wall to crumble.

Never, ever dampen the optimism and ideas that flow so freely from your child. Instead, help him find ways to apply his ideas judiciously toward practical solutions.

DAYDREAMERS
How many of you remember the first report card indicating that your child was daydreaming during class? And wasn't our first instinct to "put an end to that"? Not so fast. The imagination can be a powerful source of energy, ideas and motivation. Many of our greatest athletes and entrepreneurs visualize their success using daydreams.

Where do you think Beethoven was when he daydreamed in class? He was composing beautiful music inside his head. Where do you think Monet was when his teachers tried to focus his attention on mathematics? He was creating a revolutionary impressionistic painting style.

The same people who hang his paintings on their office walls today would have labeled Monet with a disorder because his brain didn't work in a "normal" manner.

Encourage your child to use his daydreams as a creative way to build specific action plans for the future, not just as an escape. Capture those plans on paper.

DOERS PRONE TO ACTION, NOT LISTENING

Our kids are doers, not listeners. Many have auditory processing issues that can cause significant impediments in school—can you imagine listening to a teacher for six hours a day when connecting spoken words is difficult?

This is sometimes the reason parents get frustrated—we think our child is willfully disobeying or ignoring us when we give instructions. Realize that kids with ADHD have a lot of noise and ideas swirling through their minds. Make eye contact, have your child repeat instructions back to you.

Encourage your child's teacher to use visual aids and hands-on activities. Let your child pursue independent, experiential learning. *Don't lecture me for 45 minutes how to do a math problem. Show me once, then give me the assignment and let me figure it out.*

While we sometimes wish our kids were compliant listeners, we should celebrate the fact that our kids are doers and leaders. The compliant listeners often live life with the common regret, "I wish I had pursued that idea."

Our kids will live with no such regrets. They are the ones who take action and make things happen. They are not content to passively observe life pass them by—they will experience it.

Other kids read about theories in textbooks. Our kids test those theories.

Learn to harness this quality in your child. Engage him in his passions and provide a constructive focus for his energy.

Don't let your own nature limit theirs. We need doers.

CHANGE AGENTS, CHALLENGERS, RISK-TAKERS

How many times have you asked your child in frustration:

> Why do you have to question everything I say? Why can't you do things the way they are supposed to be done?

Kids with ADHD are always pushing the limits, trying new things, challenging the established norms. They do not do it, usually, to be difficult. Nor do they do it in a cynical way. They simply see the world through different lenses than you do. It is natural and normal, albeit frustrating.

It gets them in trouble with bosses, teachers, parents and other authority figures who don't understand that their questioning is not a personal challenge, but rather a serious search to discover better ways to do things.

These very qualities—combined with a certain steadfastness, perseverance and creativity—are responsible for breakthroughs in the arts, sciences and business world. Can you see how these qualities would be required in many professions?

Instead of becoming defensive or fighting your child's nature, learn to anticipate circumstances in which he is prone to question or push the limits. Seek to understand what he is ultimately attempting to learn or do, then teach him more constructive ways to achieve the same goal.

ENERGY, HYPERFOCUS, HYPERACTIVITY

Our daughter wakes up with a glimmer in her eye, eager to take on the day. She's as bright as sunshine, but never stops. This often leaves her restless and cranky. Some days she can't focus enough to complete a single page of work. But when she is interested in a subject, a tornado could not distract her. Over time, we've learned to harness this energy, tie it to her larger goals and help her complete her work in waves.

--Dale and Julie H.

My son should replace the Energizer Bunny. He doesn't need batteries, he's always fully charged. His mind never stops, and though that used to bother us, we've begun to help channel that energy. He plays sports year-round, which gives him an outlet for his physical energy. We try to keep the environment at home peaceful and uncluttered, which allows him downtime to get refreshed. It also allows his mind to continue churning out ideas without producing chaos—we talk about the ideas and evaluate them together so that he can learn which ideas have promise and which do not.

--Michelle D.

Our kids, for the most part, do not have attention deficit. They have attention inconsistency. How can the same child who can't focus for five minutes on a math problem later spend four hours uninterrupted on a project he's interested in? Parents are naturally confused by this contradiction.

Your child cannot remember a simple assignment from school, but can recall the exact horsepower of 25 different sports cars and pinpoint the length of runway necessary for various airplanes to take off and land.

Our kids' ability to hyperfocus on gifts and passions—subjects they are interested in—helps them overcome obstacles to achieve large goals. The challenge is to tie learning of specific skills and subjects to their goals and passions.

Children with ADHD can wear you down quickly. Learn to funnel the physical, intellectual and emotional energy into activities with structure and clear parameters.

Never seek to diminish this energy. It is a gift. Harness it. Capitalize on it. And enjoy it. One thing we can agree on—our kids are never predictable or boring!

INDEPENDENT LEARNERS AND WORKERS

Many parents are concerned because their children seem too independent. Many people with ADHD prefer experiential learning and would rather work alone. Working with others can cause confusion and disruption of their rhythm. Provide opportunities for independent learning.

Creative people who write, create music or paint need significant alone time. They are most often quite content in their world of ideas.

Do not be concerned if your child has fewer, but closer friendships—this is natural. They prefer more intimate environments, fade into the background in large groups and seek out one-on-one discussions.

Tell your child it's okay to have fewer friendships and that he doesn't have to be the most popular kid in the class. His inner contentment is most important.

Allow your child space to reflect, rejuvenate and think, but also encourage him to build new friendships in smaller social settings.

OPPORTUNISTIC, MOMENTUM WORKERS

Most of us want the child who works consistently, methodically and rigorously in school. It's so much easier that way (for us!).

But we have the child who works in spurts. His ability to concentrate ebbs and flows like the tides. One day he is unable to finish a short assignment; the next day, he can complete a week's worth of work, combining unbridled energy and momentum in a torrent of adrenaline.

When a child with ADHD has an important goal within reach, his adrenaline kicks into overdrive. We believe this adrenaline rush can act as a natural stimulant that mirrors the effects of common medications. It is why people with ADHD can work for days on end without much sleep when they are energized by a project. It gives them the fortitude and concentration necessary to overcome difficulties in processing.

While inconsistency can frustrate us as parents, let's learn to capitalize on this advantage and work with our child's natural flows. See if there is a rhythm to his work. Does he work better in the afternoon or evening? Are there specific triggers that make the atmosphere conducive to thinking? Help your child understand how to capitalize on his momentum to achieve his goals.

PERSISTENT, OBSTINATE, DEFIANT, CONTRARIAN, RESILIENT

Many parents nod their heads vigorously when we mention these traits. They've seen it firsthand, experienced its intensity. But let's consider the many reasons these are advantageous qualities when applied judiciously.

> My son is one of the most resolute people I've ever known. He knows what he wants and how he wants something done. This obstinate nature can be frustrating and inflexible. But at the same time, it has fostered a certain tenacity in him. My son will not be a follower. He will not succumb to peer pressure easily.
> --David R.

In fact, it is this very tenacity and defiance that makes entrepreneurs, innovators and revolutionaries successful. They absolutely must have the following attitude: "If you say I can't do it, I will prove you wrong and do it anyway." How many people have the resilience to brush themselves off after they fail, and try again? Our kids have those qualities.

> We fought my son from the day he was born. Then you challenged us to see him differently. We remembered the parable Jesus told of the man who had two sons. One was compliant to the father's face, but then did the opposite of what he promised. The other son was initially defiant, but ultimately obeyed his father. After years of struggle, we are grateful for a strong-willed child. We always know where our child stands and can talk to him openly rather than worry that he will sneak behind our backs like his friends do.
> --Carly G.

Think of all the circumstances in life in which you need someone who is tenacious, resolute and unwavering. Parents, be grateful for these qualities and view them from the broader perspective. Learn to channel them to help your kids overcome obstacles and bounce back from adversity.

Sometimes our children use these qualities to get a reaction from us. Teach your child to focus their defiance and persistence on challenging tasks and projects, not on people.

We need kids with ADHD. They are the trailblazers of the future.

DISTRACTED, SENSITIVE TO SURROUNDINGS

There is a biological and physiological basis for the distractibility of children with ADHD. But most people interpret this distractibility through an entirely negative prism— primarily because it inhibits completion of assignments and school performance.

We celebrate children with ADHD because they are wired purposefully to be very sensitive to their surroundings. Because they are "feelers" who absorb their environment—it's like they have antennae picking up on subtle senses—they are prone to distraction. In many kids with ADHD, every sense they have operates on heightened levels.

No doubt you have noted with some consternation your child's sensitivity to smell, taste or even the feel of their clothes. They will choose the comfort of fleece over style anytime. And they often will smell things that you can't. What may seem like background noise to you can sound like a rock concert playing in their head.

They are also sensitive on an emotional level. Our kids use their intuition and empathy to sense underlying feelings of sadness or despair. While they often have difficulty processing verbal instructions, they can watch two people having a discussion from afar and tell what the people are "feeling" even when they cannot hear them speak. They "feel" experiences.

It is amazing how many parents tell us their kids like to help other children with disabilities—it is because they are sensitive to others' pain and sadness.

Have you ever noticed how many actors, writers, musicians, singers, painters and poets have ADHD? They are feelers who soak up emotions. It is this highly sensitive quality that enables them to connect with people through their creative gift.

Think of the times you have heard a song that struck a chord inside—and you thought, how did that singer know that's exactly how I am feeling? Or you've looked at a painting that has an ethereal quality that captures some hidden dimension you can feel, but can't see.

The best advertising is created by people who can connect emotionally with consumers. Brand Managers use this insight to identify unmet consumer needs and develop new products.

The very same quality that causes distraction in school is often our kids' greatest gift as well. It is responsible for the empathy that often pours from their hearts.

Proactively encourage this sensitivity. Teach your child how to use these gifts to help others and pursue his passions.

When it is time for your child to study, try to create an environment conducive to thinking. Each child is different.

One may prefer a small, uncluttered space where it is completely quiet. Some may prefer subtle background noise to drown out other noises. Try running a fan in your child's room if he has trouble concentrating on work. Others may prefer to study in a mall food court feeding off the energy around them.

Learn how your child experiences the world around him. It is probably much different than the way you experience the world.

ACTION PLAN # 5: TURN NEGATIVES INTO POSITIVES

Create a plan to systematically turn each negative tendency into a positive. Some will take longer than others. Help your child to become self-aware and explain how his unique wiring can be powerful when applied constructively.

TAKE A FRESH LOOK WHILE YOUR CHILD IS SLEEPING

I look at other people's kids who are compliant, excel in school and are sailing through childhood. And I really like those kids, I do. At one point, I wanted a child like that and wished I had an easy kid at home. But now?

I wrote the following one night after peeking in at my son sleeping. I encourage you to do the same. I hope you will discover some common feelings toward your child.

I peek in at him late at night lying in bed, fast asleep, my no-longer-little guy sprawled out across his bed, long unruly mess of hair covering his face...and I smile. I smile because he is full of personality. He is so different than me in many ways, different than my expectations, different than the little boy I had always imagined. And for that I am grateful. He's his own person, knows what he likes and doesn't like. I look in at him, peaceful and innocent while he sleeps. The fight is gone and his little mind is resting. He's gone full force for the last sixteen hours, he needs a break.

I like it that he pushes the limits, like it that he questions everything, because one day he's going to do something spectacular. Along the way, he's going to make some big mistakes, but he's going to live large and dream large. Underneath the spunk and mouth is a heart not only lined with gold, but filled with it. It is large and feeling, and it wants to do good even when his impulses lead him astray at times.

I think God must look down and confuse him with a little tornado. But I also think God looks down and likes what he has created, likes the little tornado who is growing into a man.

I think He sees Himself in my little boy, funny as that sounds. The part of God who is the Creator, who by the sheer force of His energy and being created life and all that is in the world. The part of God who was willing to step into humanity and persevere on a rugged cross because it would help people. The part of God who walked among men, largely misunderstood, often reviled because He was different and didn't do things the way the rulers of His era thought they should be done.

But He kept going. Because He, too, had a mission. He didn't care what others thought. His vision was larger than a mere thirty-three years on earth.

I think God must see Himself in the part that sometimes misses out on earthly things because he's in tune with something deep inside another person. The part who remains an idealist even when the world around him is less than ideal. The part that isn't afraid to look into eternity and see better things in all of us.

That is my son sleeping there. We fought each other until we couldn't fight anymore. Until I realized that I was the one who needed to change, because I wasn't going to change his nature. Perhaps he has been given to me so that I would change.

That is my son. He makes me angry sometimes, makes me frustrated. Then he makes me laugh, even smile in resignation. And as I look at him, he makes me cry. He is a wonderful creation. Through all the struggle, I can see the imprints of the Creator.

He is my son. He marches to the beat of a different drummer. Thank God.

6 DEVELOP THEIR NATURAL GIFTS, TALENTS AND PASSIONS

We celebrate children with ADHD because developing their gifts, talents and passions restores confidence, purpose and joy.

Our simple three-step action plan to help children with ADHD thrive is to:

I. FIND THEIR GIFTS AND PASSIONS

Children with ADHD are wired differently, on purpose. So let's identify their natural gifts, talents and passions.

II. FOSTER THEIR GIFTS AND PASSIONS

Cultivate your child's gifts, talents and passions.

III. FOCUS ON THEIR GIFTS AND PASSIONS

Develop a systematic, written plan to strengthen your child's body, soul and spirit. Provide the resources and accountability necessary to develop his gifts and passions.

STEP 1: DISCOVER THE TRAILBLAZER WITHIN— FIND YOUR CHILD'S GIFTS AND PASSIONS

DEFINITIONS

Gifts are the innate skills or abilities our children are born with. They are usually associated with creative efforts or athletics. "She is a gifted singer, he is a gifted pitcher." Gifts are bestowed, whether by genetics or a special dispensation from the Creator. They can be enhanced and developed by practice, but no amount of effort by an individual can "create" a gift.

Talents and abilities are specific tasks, actions or behaviors a person is skilled at doing. Talents can be learned, and with dedicated effort, people can become proficient in many fields.

Passions are an indescribable affinity for a vocation or cause. Passions can be given from birth or formed by exposure to meaningful events or inspirational people. Some have a passion to help the poor, work with disabled children or save the environment. Other people have a passion for sports, creative endeavors or exploration.

Passions are not always linked to a natural ability. A person may have a passion for flying, but need special instruction to fulfill that passion.

10 TRUTHS ABOUT GIFTS AND PASSIONS

1. Everyone has gifts, talents and passions. Watch and listen carefully to discover them.

2. Children with ADHD are purposefully wired with different gifts and passions.

3. Working with a child's natural wiring, rather than against it, proves most fruitful.

4. Gifts, talents and passions are powerful because they originate from inside a person—they are part of his being.

5. People feel satisfied and complete when expressing their gifts, talents and passions.

6. Gifts are often evident from an early age. "I knew when I was eight-years-old that I wanted to be a firefighter."

7. Gifts and passions can be discovered by finding where your child *is* when he daydreams, not by chastising him.

8. Follow your child's roadmap—note his natural inclinations and gifts. Hint: the very qualities that drive you crazy...will provide clues to finding his gifts and passions.

9. These gifts, talents are passions are inside for a reason. "I don't know why, I've just always loved helping kids."

10. Some people describe their gifts as a calling. It is something that has chosen them, rather than something they have purposefully tried to develop.

COMMON METHODS OF DISCOVERY

In many cases, a child's gifts are obvious. Other times, you must observe and probe as their gifts develop over time.

Observation

Do what you normally do as a parent—watch your children play, watch them work. Follow your child's roadmap and see where he takes you. You will often see his natural inclinations toward activities or subjects that fascinate him.

Does your child play with blocks? Is he constantly building elaborate structures or airplanes, or stages upon which to perform? Does your child inevitably gravitate toward creative pursuits whenever she has the chance? Does he always want books on firefighters or enjoy visiting museums with ancient artifacts and dinosaurs?

> We noticed that Ben was interested in building from a young age. He followed my husband to the garage every weekend, watching him work, using his own little plastic drills and hammering on wood. Over time, it became evident he was more gifted at building than my husband. He could see in three dimensions and fix things around the house quickly and intuitively.
> --Beth S.

> Our daughter Susan always wanted to watch television shows on medical procedures or hospital dramas such as ER. While other kids were playing house, she was playing Emergency Rescue. She wanted to enroll in CPR classes when she was eight. After high school, she began pre-med studies and volunteered as an EMT.
> --Jon and Kyla G.

My first funny memory of Samantha was seeing her standing on a kitchen chair covered with flour. Eggs and sugar were spilled all over the counter. In time, she became quite a baker. I missed those times with her once she started first grade, but rediscovered them during the summer. In high school, she started her own business selling baked goods. Now, she's opening a bakery and coffee bar.

--Nancy C.

Discussion

Listen. Does your child vocalize his desires and daydreams? Is she imagining herself on stage, on a ball field or in an emergency room healing patients? Never discourage daydreaming—it is a natural extension of your child's inner compass.

No matter where she was—in the car, at the dinner table, in school or in front of the television—my daughter was someplace else. We thought she was trying to escape reality. Then one night at bedtime, I asked her what she had been daydreaming about. She told me this beautiful story. The characters were real and the relationships surprisingly mature for her age. I asked if she wanted to start writing the stories down. She said she tried, but it was difficult for her to get the thoughts from head to paper. I canceled the piano classes she had always resisted and instead enlisted the help of a local writer. Slowly, she began to turn her imagination into these beautiful stories. She's a starving artist right now, but she loves what she is doing.

--Marcia T.

10 QUESTIONS TO DISCOVER GIFTS, TALENTS AND PASSIONS

1. What activities do you naturally enjoy?

2. What are you naturally skilled at doing?

3. What do you daydream about? Describe how it feels.

4. What activity makes you feel satisfied and fulfilled?

5. What idea most excites and inspires you?

6. What is it about that idea or thought that makes you feel energized or satisfied?

7. What do you care about deeply? What moves you?

8. Who do you want to be like when you grow up?

9. What are some jobs that sound exciting to you?

10. Do you have a desire to help people? If so, who and why?

STEP 2: FEED THE TRAILBLAZER WITHIN— FOSTER YOUR CHILD'S GIFTS AND PASSIONS

FEED GIFTS AND PASSIONS EARLY

Children's gifts are often evident from an early age, sometimes as young as eight-years-old. If we see a gift for playing piano, running a business or building skyscrapers—or a passion for helping people or exploring space—why do we make our children wait until they are 22 to pursue them?

Nothing in our child's nature suggests they need to proceed through 16 years of schooling before developing their gifts. Some current social theory postulates that artificially prolonging childhood causes boredom, exacerbates restlessness and leads to mischief in high school.

Ben Franklin left home at eleven to become a printer's apprentice and gained a wealth of experiences that prepared him to be an accomplished inventor, sage and statesman. Thousands of American soldiers, barely out of high school, exhibit tremendous leadership and heroism daily.

Is there anything you can do to break the focus of a 12-year-old who is passionate about a subject, cause or activity? Nothing can hold that child back. So why do we?

10 WAYS TO CULTIVATE YOUR CHILD'S GIFTS, TALENTS AND PASSIONS

1. Provide opportunities for your child to engage in activities he naturally enjoys.

2. Encourage your child to pursue interests that you don't share or that may not seem "practical." You can try to make an artist into a lawyer, but nature ultimately wins.

3. Provide specialized instruction, coaching and training. Have your child make a personal investment by contributing a small amount toward classes or tutoring.

4. Give your child an opportunity to participate in as many practices, games or competitions as possible.

5. Expose your child to experiences, museums, historical landmarks and performances where he can be inspired.

6. Surround your child with positive teachers, friends, family and mentors to provide inspiration and accountability.

7. Provide opportunities for independent learning. Help your child "own" his dream—don't make it about you.

8. Help teachers understand how your child can apply his gifts in the classroom.

9. Instead of seeking to change your child, change the way you teach him. Proactively turn negatives into positives.

10. Encourage siblings to support and help one another.

STEP THREE: BUILD THE TRAILBLAZER—FOCUS ON YOUR CHILD'S GIFTS AND PASSIONS

PROPER PERSPECTIVE

Our obsessive fixation on school as the barometer of success in our child's life is destructive. This artificial pressure compounds frustration and destroys self-confidence. School becomes an all-consuming monster that saps families' energy, peace and joy.

The primary focus of our child's life should be developing his gifts, talents and passions—this provides positive experiences and breeds confidence. School should assume its proper place—along with extracurricular activities such as sports, clubs, lessons, training and play—as one of many means to help a child achieve his dreams.

Which is ultimately more important: developing our child's gifts, talents and passions or ensuring that he tests well in school?

BUILD YOUR SNOWMAN: DEVELOP A WRITTEN PLAN

We are comprised of three parts—all equal in importance—just like a snowman. The essential elements of a human being are body, soul and spirit. In order for our child to achieve his goals, it is critical that we create a systematic, written plan to develop each of these three areas fully.

Being strong—or weak—in one dimension can impact another. Someone strong in spirit with courage and tenacity may endure longer practice sessions or workouts. Anger, frustration or other negative emotions can sap a person of physical strength.

As part of your action plan, define specific steps to achieve excellence in body, soul and spirit. Be explicit so that you can measure progress and provide accountability.

BODY—PHYSICAL

The body governs the skill with which we play an instrument or perform athletically. Musicians must spend countless hours practicing their instruments in order to excel. Athletes must spend countless hours honing their skills while developing a high level of physical fitness and stamina. Many professions require a particular precision with hands, eyes or feet.

Some require delicate skills, others raw strength, still others need both. You may need to foster a dozen different skills or develop strength in several parts of the body.

Do you want to broaden your skill set to include learning other musical instruments or playing other sports? How do you plan to go above and beyond your competition to achieve your goals?

List all the skills you need and a plan to develop each. Be specific about the amount or type of practice, exercise, training, tutoring, coaching, instruction and learning that will be required.

SOUL—MIND, WILL AND EMOTIONS

The soul is comprised of the mind, will and emotions.

Mind

Our minds represent our intellect and ability to reason. Schooling focuses almost exclusively on developing our intellect. Many professions require advanced technical or specialized knowledge through graduate study. Some amount of intelligence and aptitude for specific concepts appears genetic. But much can be learned through studying, reading and relevant experiences.

- How do you plan to gain specific knowledge necessary for success (instruction, tutoring, reading, independent learning, practice, training)?

- How do you plan to achieve the educational requirements required for success?

- Is there a specific college you want to attend? How do you plan to gain admission?

- How do you plan to attain necessary experiences (internships, apprenticeships, jobs)?

Will

A person's will consists of intangible qualities—desire, courage, determination, initiative, sacrifice. These intangible qualities are driven by internal attitudes that provide a competitive edge or help a person perform at a higher level than his physical or intellectual prowess would normally dictate.

One of my favorite maxims is, "What you do when no one is watching determines how well you do when people are watching."

- How much courage, determination and sacrifice will be required to achieve your goal? Do you possess those qualities sufficiently now? How do you plan to become stronger in these areas?

- How much are you willing to push yourself physically, mentally or emotionally?

- Who can encourage you and hold you accountable to grow in these areas?

Emotions

Our emotions can have a very powerful effect—positively or negatively—on the achievement of our child's dreams. Growing up in a stable and encouraging, yet challenging environment contributes to an emotionally-balanced life. Like many others, kids with ADHD can tend toward extremes. The fact that they are often intuitive "feelers" who are able to sense the feelings of others makes them effective as actors, artists, songwriters and performers.

- How can you channel your emotions to help you achieve your goal?

- How do you plan to temper or balance negative emotions such as anger?

- Are there positive emotions that you need to develop more fully?

SPIRIT

Our spirit is our connection to God and our larger purpose. Many people draw tremendous strength from their relationship to the One who created and designed them. This connection can have transforming power—to strengthen a person inside, make his relationships stronger, inspire selflessness and provide peace of mind.

Having a higher calling or larger purpose often enables a person to make sacrifices and choices to accomplish extraordinary goals. The clarity of thought resulting from a clear conscience and heart is immeasurable.

Because our gifts are given to us by God, we have great liberty. No one can take away our gifts and we cannot lose them. We encourage practicing gratitude and stewardship by using our gifts to benefit others.

- What part can your faith play in achieving your goal?

- Have you prayed for wisdom to understand and achieve your purpose?

- Are there character traits that would help you achieve your goal? How can you apply your faith to develop these traits further?

- How can you use your gifts to benefit others?

DEFINE MEASURABLE PROGRESS POINTS

Now that we have a written plan in place, we must define measurable progress points and continually evaluate our child's progress against his goals.

Our primary concern should not be, "How is my child doing in school?" Rather, our primary question should be, "How is my child progressing in developing his gifts, talents and passions?"

Determine a specific timetable to measure each goal.

- How will you know if your child is progressing and when he has succeeded?

- Break your child's goals into smaller parts so that he can achieve a series of wins along the way.

- Continually reassess and refine specific objectives or action steps every three months.

- As your child masters skills, find new areas to develop.

Together, you can use your action plan as a living, evolving guidepost.

PROVIDE THE NECESSARY RESOURCES

Our best intentions will be meaningless if we do not provide the resources necessary to develop our child's skills and passions. Even though financial resources can impact the quality and quantity of training and education, it is important that our children understand how to compensate for deficiencies and develop the intangibles that provide a competitive advantage.

More than anything, our children need our consistent, positive emotional encouragement.

ACTION ITEM # 6: DEVELOP YOUR CHILD'S GIFTS, TALENTS AND PASSIONS

A. Identify your child's gifts, talents and passions.

B. List specific ways you can help cultivate those gifts and passions.

C. Develop a written plan to achieve excellence in body, soul and spirit.

D. Define measurable progress points and refine your child's plan continually. "How is my child progressing in developing his gifts, talents and passions?"

E. List the financial, experiential and emotional resources you can provide your child.

7 CRAFT A VISION WITH LARGE GOALS

We celebrate children with ADHD because they are idealistic, world-changers whose larger vision helps curb short-term, impulsive behavior.

A FIREMAN OR MOVIE STAR?
What does your child want to be when he grows up? How does he want to express the gifts and passions you have identified?

Maybe your daughter has told you a thousand times she is going to sing on Broadway or become a CEO. Perhaps you have noticed patterns over time that will give you clues—your child consistently watches documentaries, goes to museums and reads about a particular subject in his spare time.

Allow their dreams to stay broad and flexible. Your child may demonstrate a genuine passion for building, beginning with LEGOs. He could be an engineer, an architect or a builder.

If your child hasn't expressed his desires, draw him out. If he could make a movie, how would his life unfold on the big screen—ask him to describe the title, plot and characters.

Each child is different. Their goals may surprise you. They may be modest (to own a florist shop) or grandiose (be the first man on Mars).

The important first step is to feed that curiosity and expose your child to different avenues for using his gifts. He will naturally gravitate to particular interests over time.

EXAMPLES OF LARGER GOALS

The list is endless. The following are a few examples:

Performing Arts
Perform on Broadway or at Carnegie Hall
Write screenplays, novels or songs
Star in movies or record music
Paint, sculpt, create

Science, Engineering and Exploration
Invent new products
Design cars, rockets or buildings
Fly airplanes
Practice medicine, veterinarian

Sports
Compete in the Olympics
Play college or professional sports
Coach or own a team

Business
Start and run a business as an entrepreneur
Manage a large corporation as executive
Sell stocks, cars or other products

Philanthropy
Feed the hungry in third-world countries
Help children or the elderly
Develop a ministry for people in prison

Do not limit your child—he or she may have multiple gifts, talents and passions to develop.

THE PRINCIPLE OF 1,000 CHOICES

Achieving a large goal or mission in life does not happen by accident. You don't wake up one morning and unleash your gift on mankind to rousing applause.

To achieve your dreams requires a series of 1,000 individual choices made consistently for years. The smaller the choice, the easier to dismiss it. Having a larger goal or mission gives your child a reason to make the right choices.

You can choose to watch television or practice piano. You can lie around the house or train your body. You can play video games or you can study. You can eat a burger and fries or choose a healthier meal. Each is a choice.

Create a visual reminder of the 1,000 choices with your child. Pick a symbol or abbreviation that represents your child's goal. For example, type and copy the word FLY or SING so that each sheet of paper contains 100 symbols. Then copy ten sheets so that you now have 1,000 choices in a binder.

MARK YOUR PROGRESS

Make the *1,000 Choices Checklist* a visual reminder of the daily choices necessary. Have your child cross out a symbol every time he makes a good choice that impacts his dreams. Be generous, but tough. Date the top of every new page.

Seeing the pages fill up with positive choices will breed self-confidence. The sheer number of choices made over time will provide a measure of accountability. Your child will not be as likely to jeopardize all his hard work and dreams for one bad choice such as taking drugs or drinking alcohol.

CURB NEGATIVE BEHAVIORS

Actively working toward a larger vision can help mitigate many of the negative tendencies associated with ADHD.

- Impulsiveness—When children have a larger purpose, they are less likely to make impulsive, short-term decisions that can ruin their larger plan.

- Lack of focus—Our kids are capable of sustained focus when they are energized by a project or goal.

- Hyperactivity—Working toward their dreams provides an outlet for their tremendous energy.

- Difficulty in school—Children are more motivated to overcome obstacles and work hard when they see how learning can help them achieve their goals.

- Risky behavior—Many children with ADHD seek short-term thrills when they are bored. Pursuing a big dream provides an adrenaline rush and a reason not to risk their future.

- Relationships—Working toward a larger goal helps children overcome peer pressure and make good relationship choices.

ACTION PLAN # 7: CRAFT A VISION WITH LARGE GOALS

A. List your child's goals and dreams.

B. Create the 1,000 Choices Checklist.

8 LIVE WITH PURPOSE

We celebrate children with ADHD because they have giving hearts with a need to find purpose in their lives. We practice gratitude and stewardship by using our gifts to benefit others.

GIVEN FROM ABOVE

The Declaration of Independence boldly declares that we are born with certain inalienable rights granted by the Creator. This is a powerful statement, and one which the abolitionists seized upon to note that the dignity of a person is not subject to another man's opinion or influence. Rather, it is given from above and intrinsic to each person.

Likewise, the gifts that are inside our children are granted from above. This means that no person has the power to take them, and they cannot be lost. It also means that we should practice gratitude and stewardship by using these gifts to help others.

WHY DOES YOUR MOVIE MATTER?

In the inspirational film, "Chariots of Fire," Scottish missionary and Olympic runner Eric Liddell's sister, Jennie, paints him into a corner, trying to force him to make the false choice between serving God and running. Eric Liddell's response is instructive. "God made me fast, and when I run, I feel His pleasure."

Many people find satisfaction in their passions because it is what they were born to do. Linking this natural desire to an altruistic purpose provides even more meaning and satisfaction.

Children with ADHD often have great empathy for hurting people and are sensitive to those in need. If possible, they would live to make people happy.

They may have a desire—some describe it as a calling—to serve the least among them, to help children or the elderly, to help stamp out illiteracy, starvation or abuse. Encourage your child to write down ways in which he could use his gifts or talents to help others.

5 BENEFITS OF HAVING A HIGHER PURPOSE

Living beyond one's self with a higher purpose is important for several reasons.

1. It provides the satisfaction and fulfillment of doing what you were born to do.

2. Crafting a vision teaches children important life skills and traits such as discipline, goal setting, prioritizing, overcoming obstacles and decision-making.

3. The adrenaline rush of pursuing goals that are large and good serves as a natural stimulant to encourage focus and overcome obstacles.

4. Pursuing a higher purpose for the benefit of others helps subjugate short-term impulses.

5. Having a higher purpose gives meaning to life, which is ultimately energizing for people with ADHD.

GRATITUDE AND STEWARDSHIP

Your child may be familiar with one of the most memorable lines from the movie, "Spiderman." *With great power comes great responsibility.*

Show your child creative ways to use his gifts, talents and passions to help others. Experiencing the satisfaction of helping others is addictive. Research has found a correlation between giving and happiness. Giving to others also makes children feel a part of the larger whole.

Focusing attention on someone else helps children realize that others have even greater struggles. And it will provide them with the kind of meaning and satisfaction they crave.

When the struggle to achieve their dreams becomes extremely difficult, it is helpful to know inside that they aren't only fighting for themselves, they are fighting to help others.

ACTION PLAN # 8: LIVE WITH PURPOSE

A. Talk to your child about why his life matters and how he can live with a higher purpose. Make it a part of your family's own mission statement and practice. Write down ways your child can use his gifts, talents and passions to benefit others.

B. Provide opportunities for your child to serve others. Volunteer at soup kitchens, clean up your neighborhood, visit children's hospitals together. Selflessness is always an honorable virtue to practice. You can help your child understand at a young age that his life has meaning and purpose.

9 IDENTIFY AND OVERCOME OBSTACLES

We celebrate children with ADHD because they possess the fortitude to overcome obstacles. We will not allow anyone to use ADHD as an excuse to fail.

It is an absolute tenet of life that anyone trying to achieve his dreams will face seemingly insurmountable obstacles. So it is critical that we:

1. Identify potential obstacles.
2. Develop a plan to overcome those obstacles.

EVERYONE HAS OBSTACLES TO OVERCOME

Children with ADHD face legitimate, serious difficulties. So does everyone else.

Some have learning disabilities, some physical disabilities. Some have great personalities, some don't. Some people are too short, some too tall, some too chunky, some too skinny.

Some are uncoordinated, some very athletic. Others have difficulty with mechanical operations. Many must overcome racial barriers or prejudice. Some have self-esteem issues, some have diseases, some have families in complete disarray. Some face poverty and lack of opportunities.

Even those who seem to "have it all" can have debilitating character defects—pride, arrogance, selfishness, bitterness, laziness or pessimism—that can jeopardize success.

NO EXCUSES

The heart of this book is the need for unbridled enthusiasm in the face of challenges. The principles of achievement are the same for everyone: having a vision, working hard, being resourceful, overcoming obstacles and maintaining a grateful attitude.

We must be cautious not to allow ourselves to feel "special" or wallow in self-pity or victimization. The overwhelming negativity associated with ADHD is sometimes more destructive than the actual affects of ADHD itself. This negativity can squelch the inner passion of our children.

A very special quality our kids possess is an overcoming spirit, the willingness to fight. They can be stubborn and strong-willed, and this fortitude can be tremendously beneficial.

ACTION PLAN # 9: IDENTIFY AND OVERCOME OBSTACLES

A. First, work with your child to identify potential obstacles—in body, soul and spirit—to his success.

BODY
Poor physical fitness or diet
Inadequate physical skills

SOUL
Lack of confidence, courage, will or determination
Lack of knowledge or specialized training
Destructive relationships

SPIRIT
Selfishness, arrogance, pride
Peer pressure, poor choices—drug or alcohol use

B. Now work with your child to develop a specific plan to overcome each of his obstacles.
   - Surround yourself with positive friends and peers.
   - Do not put yourself in compromising situations.
   - Take advantage of specialized training.
   - Encourage accountability to mentors or instructors.
   - Gain strength of character and virtues by becoming active in a church youth group.
   - Create a family exercise and diet plan to hold each other accountable.
   - Develop small, specific goals that can be measured over time. Set up a reward system for achieving specific goals that require you to push yourself.

Nothing can stand in our way, except ourselves.

10 ENCOURAGE HEALTHY RELATIONSHIPS

We celebrate children with ADHD because they are content inside and possess the compassion necessary to forge intimate relationships.

10 STRATEGIES TO IMPROVE RELATIONSHIPS

Parents lie awake at night worrying that their child does not have many friends...even while their own relationships at home are strained.

Appearances can be deceiving. Sometimes the most popular kids need to be around others because they can't stand to be alone. The fact is that many of our kids are very content inside.

Because our kids tend to be more creative and in tune with their inner thoughts and imagination, they are sometimes less in tune with other kids. They are content within and, therefore, not as dependent on others.

At the same time, they are also empathetic and compassionate. These are great qualities essential for intimate relationships.

Following are ten strategies to help your child forge more intimate relationships with others...and to help you and your child develop a healthier relationship at home.

1. FEED YOUR CHILD HEAPING SPOONFULS OF POSITIVE AFFIRMATION

Many children with ADHD are accustomed to hearing negative reinforcement all day. Sometime the only attention they receive is in response to undesired behaviors.

If you want to completely change your relationship with your child, be proactive in giving praise for positive behavior instead of reacting disapprovingly to negative behavior.

Show more enthusiasm for his good behavior than displeasure for bad behavior. Prevent him from acting out by giving your energy to what he is doing right, and for making progress.

Words are powerful. Greet your child with a smile and kind words in the morning. After school, tell him you are proud of him for the progress he's made. Pray for him when you tuck him into bed. Thank God out loud for his good qualities.

Believe in your child and help him *live up to high expectations* rather than down to low expectations. Children with ADHD like to please and hunger to excel.

Create a climate of success. Give your child opportunities to feel good about improving poor behavior and making positive strides. Offer kind words, hugs, or small prizes for reaching specific goals. Aim for slow progress rather than instant results. A series of small wins can build momentum and confidence.

Heaping positive affirmation will begin to change you inside—you will see your child in a different light. And so will your child. You will find a transformed child who derives satisfaction and pleasure from living up to high expectations.

2. BUILD SELF-CONFIDENCE

Parents sending their child to our Trailblazers™ Creativity Camp usually have two goals: to build their child's confidence and foster new friendships. The two go hand in hand.

How many times have you heard your child say, "Mom, I'm different than other kids. I don't fit in." Nothing breaks your heart more. They are not the popular kids and they know it.

With everyone saying "there is something wrong with you," it is no wonder our children lack confidence. Before they can feel comfortable reaching out to others, they need to first like themselves.

Focusing on gifts and passions is essential to build your child's self-confidence. Create a climate of success so he can experience the satisfaction of achievement. You must also let your child know that he's okay as he is and that it is perfectly fine to have a few really close friends that are important to him.

3. EMPOWER YOUR CHILD

Learning how to develop friendships is no different than learning how to add, subtract, multiply and divide. It is a skill that you need to teach your child.

Start by modeling appropriate relationships with your spouse, children and friends. Your child will observe you carefully. If you are always negative toward your child, how can you expect him to treat classmates any differently? If we constantly try to fix what is wrong, we will never have time to focus on the positives.

Empower your child by teaching him how to use his intuition to read body language. Our kids can learn to recognize social cues that even others don't see because they are incredibly perceptive.

Kids with ADHD also need to understand that they are often an enigma to others. At times, our kids can be incredibly engaging—they are funny and warm and animated. But a few minutes later, they can shut out the world and withdraw within themselves to process what they are feeling or simply feel rejuvenated.

These seeming contradictions in personality can confuse other people who don't "get" them, causing misunderstandings and hurt feelings.

Unfortunately, others may interpret this behavior as being aloof or snobby. A vicious cycle then begins. Other kids sensing this distance may not invite them to be part of their group, which further insulates our children and causes hurt feelings.

First, both you and your child need to understand that there is absolutely nothing wrong with possessing these disparate qualities. They are a natural part of who our kids are, and each has its place. Do not try to force your child to be overly social or interactive when he needs alone time.

At the same time, we need to teach our kids to understand how their subtle attitudes can sometimes confuse or push others away. This will help them understand that other kids aren't picking on them or excluding them. They may simply be confused about which child—the engaged, animated one or the one immersed within himself—is there in the moment.

4. ENCOURAGE RELATIONSHIPS BASED ON SHARED PASSIONS

Have you observed your child with larger groups of kids? He may be the one standing against the wall or on the outer edges, looking in.

Large groups are more difficult to negotiate. Because many kids with ADHD have auditory processing issues, they feel awkward when they cannot easily follow the flow of the conversation or get jokes. They seem to get lost in the crowd and are not as quick on their feet.

Many kids with ADHD prefer to have fewer friendships. Though they may not grow up to be social butterflies, they can be incredibly intimate and vulnerable with the few people they choose to bond with.

This is an important point. Relationships are a choice. As with clothes, our kids can be very particular in picking their friends. They do not always extend the social graces to "put up" with someone they don't like. They can exhibit a take-it-or-leave-it attitude, which isn't always a bad thing. Many tend to be adept at sizing up kids you may not want them hanging out with!

Adults form relationships based on shared passions and interests. So do the same with your kids. Encourage them to get involved with extracurricular clubs, sports teams and organizations where they share common passions and interests with others.

5. "RELATIONSHIPS ARE MORE IMPORTANT THAN BEING RIGHT."

Our kids often sabotage relationships because they have a strong sense of internal justice—they need to correct wrongs and prove that they are right, often at the cost of relationships.

No one wants to be around a know-it-all or an overbearing person arguing their point into the ground. So teach your child this mantra until it becomes part of him: "Relationships are more important than being right."

6. SET EXPECTATIONS, MAKE TRANSITIONS EASIER

Adults have a great degree of control over their lives—where they work, where they live, what they have for dinner. Children must *react* to events around them. Because many kids with ADHD have difficulty transitioning, World War III often erupts when plans unexpectedly change.

Kids with ADHD can become hyperfocused and emotionally invested in an activity they are looking forward to such as being with a friend or attending an event. When, at the last minute, we change plans without telling them, you know what happens!

So, set expectations ahead of time. "Ryan, I want to set expectations about tonight. I want you to be able to stay at Jimmy's house until ten, but we will most likely need to leave by eight. If we can stay later, then that's a bonus."

Also make sure your child understands clear consequences for actions. Sometimes your child will say he didn't hear you. Look him in the eyes and ensure you have his undivided attention.

7. REDUCE STRESSORS

You know your child's hot buttons, situations that push him over the edge. Do him—and yourself—a favor. Don't expose your child to situations that expose negatives and weaknesses. Millions of people do this daily. How many people struggling with their weight avoid Dunkin Donuts? How many people who have asthma avoid smoky bars?

We make rational decisions every day to reduce stressors in our lives. We take a different road and choose fast food for dinner.

When Santa is bringing my son a new bike, I have two options. I can attempt with grand futility to assemble the bike myself, therefore ensuring that I ruin the Christmas spirit. Or I can pay the store $15 to assemble it. It's worth the fifteen dollars!

Give your child plenty of time to prepare for new situations or changes in plans. Sometimes they can handle the big stressors in life with ease, but smaller distractions and unexpected changes can cause great frustration and meltdowns.

Manage your child's homework load. Don't be afraid to say no to excessive work. Don't pick fights over issues that are inconsequential in the long run. Your child's heart is much more important than what he wears.

Provide the stability that kids with ADHD crave. Create family traditions, eat meals together, spend time in nature—in addition to clearing the mind, the order and tranquility in nature can be comforting. Encourage your child to be responsible for a family pet. Caring for a dog can help teach your child how to nurture and care for others. As always, play to your child's strengths and work with his wiring.

8.   MAKE   HOME   AN   ADHD-FRIENDLY ENVIRONMENT

Why do children who thrive on spontaneity also have an overwhelming need for order and routine?

Actually, the two work together. Because their minds are constantly swirling with ideas and some measure of disorder, our kids need the other things in their lives—from relationships to physical environment to the minute details of daily life—to be orderly. Otherwise, their entire world would become one spinning globe.

Keep paper and pencils all over the house. Encourage your child to write down his thoughts and ideas, to become a habitual note-maker. Use charts and checklists to track progress with homework or chores. Keep instructions brief. Offer frequent, friendly reminders. Limit lectures and verbal instruction. Use analogies to teach.

Keep the time that your child wakes up, eats, showers, leaves for school, and goes to sleep the same each day. If your child has specific places to keep his schoolwork, toys, and clothes, he is less likely to lose them. Save a spot near the front door for his school backpack so he can grab it on the way out the door. Keeping your home neat and pleasant can give your child a feeling of peace and contentment.

If they can count on you to help organize and take care of the little things, you can count on them to keep your life spontaneous and fun!

9. PUT ASIDE YOUR OWN EXPECTATIONS

One sentence should suffice. Let your child be himself instead of who you want him to be.

10. ENJOY YOUR CHILD

Too often we get so caught in the trap of trying to raise, teach, discipline, encourage and educate our children that we forget the most fundamental thing we can do for our kids.

Enjoy them.

ACTION PLAN # 10: ENCOURAGE HEALTHY RELATIONSHIPS

Review the ten strategies in this chapter and make a list of specific ways you can help your child enjoy healthy relationships with friends, adults…and you!

CREATE YOUR MASTER ACTION PLAN

It is critical that you take the time to complete the following Action Plan. To a large degree, this should be a collaborative effort with your child. Get him excited about his future!

Completing this Action Plan will transform you, your attitude and your child.

#1: Think Different, Wonderfully Different
List ten character attributes and traits that make your child wonderfully different.

2: Celebrate Trailblazing Qualities
List your child's trailblazing qualities.

3: Celebrate Competitive Advantages
List the advantageous qualities and competitive advantages your child possesses.

4: Capitalize on Future Trends
List ways that your child can capitalize on future trends.

5: Turn Negatives into Positives
Create a plan to systematically turn each negative tendency into a positive.

6: Develop Your Child's Gifts, Talents and Passions
A. Identify your child's gifts, talents and passions.
B. List specific ways you can help cultivate those gifts and passions.
C. Develop a written plan to achieve excellence in body, soul and spirit.
D. Define measurable progress points.
E. Provide financial, experiential and emotional resources for your child.

7: Craft a Vision with Large Goals
List your child's goals and dreams. What would a movie of his life look like?

Create the 1,000 Choices Checklist.

8: Live with Purpose
List ways your child can use his gifts, talents and passions to benefit others.

Provide opportunities for your child to serve others.

9: Identify and Overcome Obstacles
Identify potential obstacles—in body, soul and spirit—to your child's success.

Develop a specific plan to overcome each of his obstacles.

10: Encourage Healthy Relationships
List ways you can help your child enjoy healthy relationships with friends, adults…and you!

IV.

10 Strategies to Improve Your Child's School Experience

10 STRATEGIES TO IMPROVE YOUR CHILD'S SCHOOL EXPERIENCE

No obstacle represents a greater challenge than the difficulty our kids experience in school. School can be a tremendous resource for our children, so we need to know how to maximize its effectiveness while limiting negative effects.

1. KEEP PROPER PERSPECTIVE AND RELAX

We all want our children to grow up to be responsible, caring adults strong in body, soul and spirit.

Schools influence only one aspect of your child—the mind—and contribute to the acquisition of knowledge. The goal of an education is to foster curiosity, a love of learning and the ability to think. Equally as important to your child's education is teaching life skills through daily interactions and participation in extracurricular activities.

Success in school is not a predictor of success in life. Some kids struggle in school, but thrive in college when independent learning is required. Some kids are wired to bypass college and start their own entrepreneurial ventures.

School pressures often needlessly aggravate the symptoms of ADHD. Maintain your focus on developing your child's gifts, talents and passions toward a larger goal.

School is simply one means of educating your child and developing his skills. Do not allow it to become an all-consuming force that drains you and your child of energy, peace and joy.

2. BE YOUR CHILD'S ADVOCATE

Parents, you must take charge of your child's education. You are your child's primary advocate.

Do not relinquish raising and educating your child to others. We respect teachers, psychologists, psychiatrists and learning specialists for their outstanding contributions. You may be tempted to defer to professionals, but recognize that they are fallible and subject to biases. If well-meaning professionals recommend treatments that make you uneasy, challenge them.

Occasionally, you will need to say, "No!" to unnecessary homework, especially when your child already understands the concept. If you think your child needs to enjoy an extracurricular activity or take a break instead of doing his homework, don't be afraid to say so. You are not going to make your child soft. You are preserving a balanced childhood.

Parents, trust your instincts. Watch your child, listen to him. You know your child better than anyone. You must be his advocate, the one person who remains positive and excited about his future, even through struggles and doubts.

When in doubt, fight structures and systems, not your child. Fight for him, not against him.

3. GET PROFESSIONAL HELP FOR SPECIFIC ISSUES

Many children with ADHD have difficulties processing and/or recalling information. Their wiring makes it difficult to gather information, organize it and process it effectively, especially when it is communicated orally. Imagine how this difficulty is compounded when a child sits for hours listening to auditory instruction.

We do not dismiss the opinions of professionals or ignore reality. In fact, we propose a head-on approach to finding solutions.

We do advocate a judicious use of testing and professional help. Be wary of over-analyzing your child and having him visit multiple professionals to fix an endless stream of weaknesses. It is destructive to spend an inordinate amount of time trying to correct each of your child's deficiencies. So choose the most important skills that can be developed and improved in a positive manner.

Above all, focus more on your child's strengths than weaknesses.

The bottom line is this: getting professional help should reduce your child's frustration, not increase it…and increase his self-confidence, not destroy it.

4. PROVIDE TEACHERS WITH DIRECTION

Meet with teachers before the school year begins—and frequently throughout the year—to set expectations and express what your child needs to succeed.

- Be positive and offer consistent encouragement. Build on small, consistent wins. Achievement breeds confidence.
- Incorporate your child's gifts and passions into class discussions and lesson plans.
- Actively involve your child in class. Make him feel needed. Can he hand out assignments, prepare activities or share his talents to build confidence?
- Sit your child in front of the classroom to help him focus and stay involved.
- Modify your teaching style to complement the child's learning style. Use experiential, hands-on activities and visual aids. Keep instructions short.
- Allow flexibility in assignment content. Can your child complete his book report or project focusing on a topic he is passionate about?
- Allow flexibility in time necessary to complete assignments. Your child should never miss recess because he processes information more slowly.
- The purpose of tests is to measure the child's understanding of the material. Can the child take the test in a quieter environment?
- Allow for independent or creative work that shows a mastery of the key concepts being taught.

Help teachers see the big picture, that you are partnering with them to help your child grow strong in body, soul and spirit.

5. ESTABLISH REALISTIC STANDARDS

Your child is probably not going to excel in every class. He may thrive when studying bugs (biology), but tune out trying to understand the periodic table (chemistry). Relax. Natural selection in life is normal—it probably means he's not going to be a chemist, but he may turn out to be an amazing biologist.

Your focus should be on developing strengths, because your child is going to spend his life pursuing things he is good at doing. If you spend all his time trying to shore up natural weaknesses, it will undermine development of his talents.

Do establish minimum performance standards. Do not accept laziness or expect failure. Even if your child has difficulty with a subject, he should be able to understand the top three or four key concepts.

Above all, take the pressure off and foster your child's curiosity and love of learning.

6. EMPOWER YOUR CHILD WITH SELF-AWARENESS AND CHOICES

Teach your child about ADHD and how it affects him. Help him begin to identify his obstacles and struggles. As his self-awareness increases, he will naturally develop effective ways to compensate for weaknesses.

He will also begin to understand his own natural rhythms and cycles. He can capitalize on the momentum when he's concentrating well, or make adjustments when he's not. He will learn to clear large blocks of time to complete activities.

Encourage your child to make changes to his habits based on his burgeoning self-awareness. Allow him to make choices, even if they aren't your particular choices. If he studies well late at night, allow him to stay up later.

Encourage his teachers to give him choices about incorporating his talents or interests into his work. There is no reason your child shouldn't be able to gain credit for reading books that interest him, as long as they are grade-appropriate in complexity and content.

Show your child you trust him by empowering him to make choices and take control of his future.

7. COMPLEMENT SCHOOL WITH ALTERNATIVE LEARNING EXPERIENCES

Do not minimize the importance of extracurricular activities such as sports, clubs and camps. These experiences teach skills and inspire qualities not learned in school—teamwork, leadership, discipline, perseverance, physical endurance, etc.

Don't sacrifice these experiences because of school pressures— learn to achieve a healthy balance. These experiences can help build confidence in relationships and provide a necessary release of energy. They can also further develop your child's natural gifts, talents and passions.

8. LINK SCHOOL TO YOUR CHILD'S LARGER VISION AND PURPOSE

Many children correctly question how school relates to real life. Since we are helping them develop their larger vision and purpose, it is especially instructive to tie their school experience to their larger vision. Show them how understanding principles of mathematics and physics is necessary to build rockets. Demonstrate how mastering grammar and spelling can help them succeed as a screenwriter.

Our kids will be more motivated when they understand how specific learning can help them achieve their larger dreams.

9. TEACH YOUR CHILD LIFE SKILLS, HELP HIM START HIS OWN BUSINESS

One of the best ways to improve your child's school experience is to make home life more enjoyable. Take time to enjoy your child and his interests. Use his gifts and passions as a springboard to teach him important life skills. By doing this, you will show him that school is not the only measure of success or source of education. You will help him be well-rounded and feel confident that he can learn and achieve.

Starting a business gives a child with ADHD another place to focus his tremendous energy and creativity. The life skills learned in developing ideas, producing a product or service, marketing and promoting the business, dealing with customers, learning about cost and revenue streams, etc. can be invaluable. Having his own business—even if it is as simple as taking care of pets, mowing lawns or babysitting—can provide a sense of confidence and control. And the business may provide an opportunity to further develop gifts, talents and passions.

10. CONSIDER HOME SCHOOLING

Do not be afraid to consider alternative options for your child. Though home schooling is not for everyone, many families are extremely excited about how it has changed their families.

Home schooling provides the flexibility kids with ADHD need. The curriculum can be customized for their particular learning style (using visual, hands-on learning tools) and work cycle (work in short bursts or carve out large chunks of uninterrupted time, either in the morning or at night, or spread out throughout the day). You can create uncluttered, quiet work spaces and allow plenty of time for independent study. The customization is virtually unlimited.

Home schooling eliminates a source of external stress for both you and your child. While it is not easy and requires tremendous sacrifice from the parents, you may find that this option completely changes your family life. Many home schooling families have been able to reduce or eliminate their child's use of stimulant medication.

Home schooling saves a tremendous amount of time. There is no need to rise before the sun to get your child to the bus stop. All the time spent on interruptions and classroom changes can be used productively and efficiently at home. Many home schooling families are able to complete a full day's worth of work by noon, leaving the afternoon for special projects, field trips, music lessons, sports or business ventures.

Home school groups have sprung up in communities all across the country, providing plenty of opportunities for socialization and group field trips. We highly recommend this approach for families that can make it work.

TIPS FOR COMPLETING HOMEWORK

Prepare

1. Take notes during class. This can help you stay focused on the material being taught.

2. Write down information on paper to help "seal" the information inside. It forces you to think again about what you are writing.

3. Incorporate the facts you are learning into a creative story in your mind. It enables you to use your creativity while focusing on the key concepts you need to know.

4. Be proactive. Rather than waiting for teachers to address issues, talk to them openly about how ADHD affects your work. Then work with them to develop solutions. They will respect your honesty and willingness to find solutions.

5. Make a short list of things you need to do each evening. Checking items off the list provides a sense of accomplishment and momentum toward completion.

6. At the end of the evening, create a short list of tasks you want to accomplish the next day. The organization and order provides peace of mind and prevents a hectic start to the next day.

7. Break down long-term projects into separate tasks to be completed according to a timetable. Track your progress with a project list posted in your work space.

Attack

1. Create an uncluttered, organized space where you enjoy completing your homework. Have all your pencils, pens, and paper readily available.

2. Complete the most difficult homework first and get it out of the way.

3. Create flashcards to study for tests. This helps you break information into smaller bites.

4. When studying for a test, read through the chapter summaries first in order to focus on the main ideas of the chapter.

5. Give yourself a deadline with a reward for completing the work on time. "If I can complete my work by 6, then I will have two hours to play basketball until it gets dark."

6. Take a short break after every completed activity to clear your mind. Step outside, eat a snack or play with your dog...then get back to work and stay on track!

7. Use study halls and idle time to get a head start on your work. Gain small victories by beating your projected deadlines for each task. Use this momentum to continue working.

TIME MANAGEMENT TIPS

Plan

1. Plan your day using a notebook, Day Planner, computer calendar or PDA. Schedule your activities for defined periods of time.

2. Keep as much routine as possible in your day. Knowing what you need to do and when you need to do it helps you accomplish more.

3. Write a To-Do list each night for what needs to be accomplished the following day.

Organize

1. Keep supplies for your chores or homework in one place. Having to reorganize yourself each day wastes time.

2. Take a few moments to organize your schoolwork after your homework is completed.

3. Create specific, separate places to keep your schoolwork, personal items, work items and keys. Get into the habit of keeping everything in its place.

4. Create a routine that you are comfortable with every day.

Prioritize

1. Turn wasted time into productive time and get a head start on your homework.

2. Prioritize your daily activities. Complete the most difficult tasks first. Get homework completed so you can enjoy more free time playing or pursuing passions you enjoy.

3. Set time limits for each task. Then make it a game or competition in order to beat that time. (Remember that completing a task correctly the first time ultimately saves time.)

4. Do not procrastinate. Give yourself a small reward (snack, time to enjoy a game, etc.) for completing each project.

5. Set specific goals. Instead of saying, "I want to complete this project sometime this week," set a specific goal: "I will complete this project on Wednesday night by 9:00." Work always expands to the time allowed.

REMEMBER THE
MOST IMPORTANT QUESTION

How is my child's heart?

ACKNOWLEDGMENTS

We are grateful for a home filled with the laughter, wisdom and warmth of our son. We love you.

We would not be where we are today without the faithful support and encouragement of our parents. You have shaped our lives more than you know.

We are thankful for the sharp pencils and soft touches of our editors, Brent Marsden and Grace Harmon. Thank you for pushing us beyond our comfort zone, while providing a safe place to land.

We can always count on Dr. Jill Casavetti for sound advice and wisdom beyond her years. We cherish Dr. Christopher Patterson's quick wit, and even quicker offers to help at a moment's notice.

Our lives have been brightened by the friendship of Howard Glasser, whose groundbreaking book changed our perspective as parents. His tireless energy and passion for helping children fulfill their destinies continually inspires us to reach for the stars.

Ron Pettiway and Mallory Starr, whose devotion to help kids society has given up on through their pioneering Charter School efforts, have proved inspiring and challenging.

A big thanks to some special friends—Spike, Caleb, Ryan, Sean, Joey and Richard—for making our first Trailblazers™ Creativity Camp so fun and meaningful. Don't ever change who you are.

Pastors Brett Andrews, Tim Jones and Rick Ruble of New Life Church help us remember what is most important in life.

To Brett, thank you for sharing ice cream and simple encouragement, and for being a great brother and uncle.

NOVELS BY KIRK MARTIN

The Gravel Drive

The Gravel Drive is a powerful, moving and unforgettable love story between a father and his son. It will challenge you to cherish each moment and know those closest to you in the smallest of ways.

The *Gravel Drive* is sensitively written, deftly engaging, and highly recommended reading.
--Midwest Book Review

Kirk donates $1.00 from each purchase of *The Gravel Drive* to the Make-A-Wish Foundation®.

Shade of the Maple

Anna Matthews left home at eighteen, a young woman rooted in small-town virtues, seeking adventure in the Green Mountains of Vermont. She found a free-spirited young man whose boundless imagination captivated her heart. Forced apart, Anna tries to build a new life.

A decade later, a series of gripping novels awaken Anna's veiled dreams, illuminating a striking disparity within her marriage. She seeks the author, but the truth she discovers will change her life. Anna is confronted with a clear choice—continue living the comfortable, but hollow American Dream or pursue her dream.

Experience a love story as large and timeless as the Vermont landscape. Share the quest of two restless people finding peace and consuming intimacy in each other. See your dreams reflected in this triumph of enduring love.

Kirk donates $1.00 from each purchase of *Shade of the Maple* to breast cancer research.

Purchase your signed copies at **www.kirkmartinbooks.com**.

GIFTED: A NOVEL

GIFTED is a timeless story of love, courage and redemption.

In the shadow of New Hampshire's granite hills, three people with little in common find their lives indelibly intertwined.

Devan McAllister is a misunderstood seventeen-year-old, a thorn to those frustrated by his ADD, yet content within. Devan lives life on the fringes of high school by choice, but suddenly finds himself at the center of a life-changing struggle.

He begins to hear classmates' thoughts and feel their emotions. Devan must overcome self-doubt when he hears the desperate cries of socialite Grace Sullivan. His dilemma escalates when he discovers a secret that threatens the school's principal.

Banished to detention, Devan finds unexpected wisdom and friendship in custodian Abraham Thompson, who helps him understand that his intuition is a gift and challenges him to live with a larger purpose.

Devan must choose whether to embrace his gift or run from it. In the end, his decision will determine whether a young girl lives to see another sunrise, and whether an aging janitor passes through the sunset of his life with no regrets.

This compelling drama will tempt you to turn the pages quickly, but the profound insight into relationships will compel you to savor each scene. An intricately woven story with richly drawn characters, GIFTED reminds us that true love is selfless, and that our weaknesses are often our greatest gifts.

A portion of the proceeds from GIFTED will benefit the critical work being done by *The Children's Success Foundation*.

Purchase your signed copies at **www.kirkmartinbooks.com**.

ABOUT CELEBRATE!ADHD®

Celebrate!ADHD envisions a world in which children with ADHD are celebrated for their unique gifts that enrich society.

Our mission is to restore confidence, purpose and joy in children with ADHD by developing their natural gifts, talents and passions.

We provide a full range of services to help children, parents and adults find success in life. Our positive, proactive solutions build confidence, improve relationships, reduce anxiety and instill a sense of purpose in families.

Personal Coaching. Just as a sports coach develops athletic skills, a personal coach develops a child's life skills. Personal coaches help prepare children and their families for success in life. Available via email, phone and in person.

Trailblazers™ Family Workshops. These day-long workshops will empower you with the tools you need to understand and develop that little trailblazer living under your roof! Contact us to bring a Trailblazers Workshop to your city.

Trailblazers™ Creativity Camps. Our three-day Camps help build your child's confidence and social skills.

Life Skills Workshops for Kids. These fun workshops will develop your child's confidence and purpose by teaching practical life skills in a hands-on environment.

School of Creativity and Entrepreneurship. Coming in 2006…a learning experience designed specifically for kids who are wired to be entrepreneurs or performing artists.

To find out more, please visit www.celebrateADHD.com
or email us at ADHDcamp@aol.com.

SUPPORT THE CHILDREN'S SUCCESS FOUNDATION

Celebrate!ADHD® is proud to donate a portion of the proceeds from this book to benefit the critical work of **The Children's Success Foundation**.

Join us in helping transform children and families for success by making a tax deductible donation to:

The Children's Success Foundation
4165 West Ironwood Hills Drive
Tucson, Arizona 85745

Or donate online @ www.difficultchild.com/success.html

The **Children's Success Foundation**, a 501(c)(3) non-profit, provides funding, program development and professional training to promote implementation of Howard Glasser's **Nurtured Heart Approach**™ around the world.

The **Nurtured Heart Approach**, originally developed for challenging children, is a powerful and proven *drug-free* method for energizing success and creating *inner wealth* for all children in their homes, schools and communities. Since 1994, thousands of parents and teachers have learned how to transform intense children into successful children and to help all children flourish.

We also strongly encourage you to read Howard Glasser's groundbreaking book, *Transforming the Difficult Child: The Nurtured Heart Approach.* This book completely changed the course of our lives as parents, and we know it will serve as a valuable tool to help nurture your child's heart.

To learn more or to participate in a helpful online Discussion Forum, visit www.difficultchild.com.